# American and NATO Veteran Reintegration

# American and NATO Veteran Reintegration

## The Trauma of Social Isolation and Cultural Chasms

Gary Senecal and MaryCatherine McDonald

LEXINGTON BOOKS
*Lanham • Boulder • New York • London*

Published by Lexington Books
An imprint of The Rowman & Littlefield Publishing Group, Inc.
4501 Forbes Boulevard, Suite 200, Lanham, Maryland 20706
www.rowman.com

6 Tinworth Street, London SE11 5AL, United Kingdom



British Library Cataloguing in Publication Information Available

**Library of Congress Cataloging-in-Publication Data**

Names: McDonald, MaryCatherine, 1981- author. | Senecal, Gary, author.
Title: American and NATO veteran reintegration : the trauma of social isolation and cultural chasms / MaryCatherine McDonald and Gary Senecal.
Description: Lanham : Lexington Books, [2021] | Includes excerpts from interviews with veterans from the United States, Canada, Great Britain, Germany, Israel, and Norway. | Includes bibliographical references and index.
Identifiers: LCCN 2021011712 (print) | LCCN 2021011713 (ebook) | ISBN 9781498591096 (cloth) | ISBN 9781498591102 (ebook)
Subjects: LCSH: Veteran reintegration. | Veterans—Mental health—United States. | North Atlantic Treaty Organization—Armed Forces—Military life. | United States—Armed Forces—Military life. | Veterans—Interviews. | Military socialization—Case studies. | Veterans—Social conditions—Case studies. | Post-traumatic stress disorder—Prevention. | Sociology, Military.
Classification: LCC UB356 .M337 2021 (print) | LCC UB356 (ebook) | DDC 362.1968/5210086970973—dc23
LC record available at https://lccn.loc.gov/2021011712
LC ebook record available at https://lccn.loc.gov/2021011713

# Contents

# Introduction

## *An American Epidemic for Veterans: Cultural Chasms and the Trauma of Social Isolation*

### PREFACE

In the aftermath of war, part of the process of surveying the damage is to consider what are called the "signature wounds," which are the combat injuries that were unexpected, and therefore could not be prevented. In World War I, mustard gas delivered in artillery shells burned and blistered the flesh of servicemembers, caused internal and external bleeding, and stripped the mucous membranes of the bronchial tubes. It rarely killed servicemembers but left them in excruciating pain for weeks. Petroleum burns from incendiary devices that spread ignited oil across the water were the signature wounds in World War II. Napalm—another petroleum-based weapon that stuck to skin and burned at temperatures upward of 1,400 degrees Fahrenheit—caused brutal burn wounds in Vietnam.

After war, the signature wounds are catalogued and studied, as learning how to manage these wounds and prevent them in the future is a key goal of military researchers. This process has been necessary and helpful, as with each subsequent war we are able to avoid things that previously left many servicemembers killed or gravely injured. For this reason, the technology of war continues to improve, and servicemembers in the wars in Iraq and Afghanistan have been able to survive injuries that would have been impossible to survive twenty years ago.

One of the signature wounds of the wars in Iraq and Afghanistan for U.S. servicemembers is posttraumatic stress disorder (PTSD). This particular wound was proved so vast and so intractable that researchers are attempting to find ways to treat and prevent this signature wound. Since 2007, Congress has appropriated upward of two billion dollars to help improve the prevention, diagnosis, and treatment of PTSD. Interventions like embedded telehealth have been implemented to help servicemembers stay deployed after traumatic experiences, and potentially curb the development of PTSD once home (Hwang et al., 2014). These interventions are a hopeful sign, as they point to a willingness on behalf of the military to accept PTSD as a legitimate wound, which certainly has not always been the case in history. However, if a wound is to be eradicated and prevented, it must first be understood. Since PTSD is a wound of war that often blossoms when one returns *home* rather than immediately within the theater of war, it is not just war that needs to be examined but the conditions that exist at home where the wound is allowed (or perhaps even encouraged) to take hold. Whether and how this is the case is what we set out to explore in this book.

It is our contention that in the quest to fully understand the trauma incurred by the wars in Iraq and Afghanistan in particular, it is necessary to examine the question cross-culturally. What are the conditions of homecoming in our own country as compared to others? In order to shed light on the conditions within our country that may be exacerbating PTSD, we must compare the reintegration experience of servicemembers in the United States with that of our North Atlantic Treaty Organization (NATO) allies. Is PTSD from these two wars as prevalent in other countries that fought alongside our servicemembers? If so, we can safely assume that the source of disorder lies squarely within the conditions of the wars themselves. If not, we must take a hard look at what we may be doing (or failing to do) within the United States both to prepare our servicemembers for combat and to welcome them home. In other words, if PTSD is the signature wound in the United States from the Iraq and Afghanistan wars, but not the signature wound in our NATO allies, this suggests that there is something *within American culture* that provides especially fertile soil for this epidemic to grow.

Data shows that American veterans suffer from PTSD (and with it, suicidality and functional impairment) at *significantly* higher rates than veterans in other countries. Although there is room for a critical assessment of the range and nature of diagnosis of PTSD (Richardson, Frueh, & Acierno, 2010), it is notable that over the last nineteen years—roughly the length of the wars in Iraq and Afghanistan—approximately 20–25 percent of American veterans who have served during this time have been diagnosed with PTSD. On average over the last nineteen years, seven American servicemembers *from just these two wars* commit suicide each day (Beynon, 2020; Shane, 2019; U.S. Department of Veteran Affairs, 2016; Vasterling, 2016; Roh, 2012; Tanielian & Jaycox, 2008).

When compared to the data from the countries of NATO allies who fought alongside Americans in Afghanistan, differences are stark. Though there are likely sociocultural factors that might contribute to these otherwise severe discrepancies (Forslund & Lindblom, 2019), these discrepancies simply cannot account for the staggering differences. For example, in Israel, between 1 percent and 8 percent of the servicemembers deployed in these two wars, as well as in various other missions in the Middle East (e.g., Gaza), have been diagnosed with PTSD (Marcia, 2018; Forslund & Lindblom, 2019). In the UK, Australia, Germany, and the Netherlands, the numbers are between 1 percent and 6 percent (Burri & Maercker, 2014; Richardson, Frueh, & Acierno, 2010; Bandelow et al., 2012). In Canada, the numbers are the closest to the United States, topping off at between 6 percent and 10 percent (Veterans Affairs Canada, 2019).

One may wonder whether these discrepancies can be explained by examining differing rates of diagnosis. Is it possible that the United States simply diagnoses PTSD at a higher rate than our NATO allies? A full examination of this question is beyond the scope of this project. However, an answer lies within the suicide data—which catches all veterans in each of these countries, regardless of whether they have been diagnosed with PTSD or not. If we move from comparing PTSD diagnoses to the suicide data of American servicemembers with that of NATO allies, the chasm is shockingly wide. For example, fifteen Israeli servicemembers committed suicide in 2017, reducing the number to eight in 2018 (Ahronheim, 2019). For American active duty servicemembers, as far as sheer data demonstrates, suicide has been a far more lethal enemy than the Taliban or Al-Qaeda over the past two decades (Giacomo, 2019). Among active duty American military personnel, 325 committed suicide in the year 2018 alone (Kime, 2019). The number balloons to 541 servicemembers if one includes Reserve and National Guard components (Lopez, 2019). After a small dip in active duty suicides in 2019, the suicide rate for 2020 is expected to surpass the rate in 2018 (LaGrone & Eckstein, 2020; Myers, 2020). To put a finer point on the data here, more American veterans commit suicide in a single day than in a full calendar year in Israel. The chasm is just as deep between the United States and other ally countries. In Canada, there were approximately fifty-four veteran suicides between 2014 and 2017 (Veterans Affairs Canada, 2019). In the United States, that number would be reached within a little over a week. In the UK, approximately 400 veterans have committed suicide between 1994 and 2015. That's about twenty suicides per *year*, a number that the United States would reach in *three days*. And in Australia, approximately fifty veterans committed suicide in 2016, again, a number that would be reached in the United States in just over a week.

To add another layer of complication to the picture, noncombat military occupation servicemembers in the United States are also susceptible to being diagnosed with PTSD as combat occupation servicemembers, leading to a changed diagnostic criterion in the field and an expansion of the concept of trauma beyond combat stressors (Armenta et al., 2018; Brockman et al., 2017;

Gore, 2016; Kintzle, 2015; National Center for PTSD, U.S. Department of Veterans Affairs, 2020; Rosbach, 2020). For example, the most recent iteration of the Diagnostic and Statistical Manual for Mental Disorders specifies that having witnessed a traumatic event is enough to count as exposure to the stressor. This means that American veterans who have not been directly exposed to live combat but have been exposed to it in training, drone warfare (which arguably *is* direct exposure), or as responders to those who have been traumatized (e.g., psychologists and other first responders on base who do not see active combat but treat its effects) can be diagnosed with PTSD. Among our NATO allies, on the other hand, PTSD diagnoses are almost exclusively found in those who have been exposed to live combat.

The question of what factors could explain these drastic discrepancies is the central examination of this book. In order to investigate this question, we interviewed forty former servicemembers from six NATO ally countries. We utilized semi-structured interviews in order to isolate some of the specific psychosocial factors within both American civilian culture and American military culture which make it more difficult for American veterans to reintegrate to civilian life after their military careers.

The interview data was analyzed using a theory-led thematic analysis methodology to isolate trends and tease out the meaning of specific repeated phrases and words. Briefly, thematic analysis (Braun & Clarke, 2006) espouses a flexible and varying theoretical framework that acknowledges the need to let the data reveal the themes that may arise. Unlike other qualitative methods such as grounded theory and phenomenology, theory-led thematic analysis begins with theory and looks to probe the presence of said theories in the participant interviews. Though some questions are structured in a similar open-ended manner to grounded theory and phenomenology, other questions are specifically tailored to inquire about previously established theory in the field (Braun & Clark, 2006). This analysis was most appropriate given our interview approach. Each interview had open-ended questions alongside questions that were directed toward certain theoretical characteristics which were salient in predicting reintegration outcomes in American veterans in contrast to NATO allies. The specific theories we inquired about are spelled out below. Our general approach was centered on the belief that an examination of American culture alongside the cultures of our NATO allies would help us further isolate and understand the factors that contribute to the tragically high number of suicides among our veterans.

It is worth pointing out that though we certainly stand by the data that we found, there are of course several limitations to our study, especially regarding the participant pool. First, we utilized snowball sampling methods to solicit participants and the only controls present in our prescreening process involved a proof of active duty service and deployment to Afghanistan from 2001 to the present time. Second, we were both physically restricted to the United States while soliciting. This geographical limitation made it challenging to solicit NATO ally participants and certainly limited the range of diversity we required for NATO allies. Third, and tied to the previous point, only one of our participants was female. Early in the study, our intention was to have a proportionate demographic representation across gender and we began recruiting American female veterans. However, it became clear to us a few months into the solicitation period that our ability to recruit female veterans from NATO ally countries for the study would put major delays on the project. After interviewing one American female veteran, we decided to only utilize male participants for the remainder of the study. Fourth, all our participants left active duty service with an honorable discharge. This places limitations on the range of reintegration experiences we were soliciting, especially as it relates to one's employment opportunities and access to healthcare after service. Finally, all participants who took part in this study were compensated; however, just the act of volunteering for 90–120-minute interviews around social reintegration experiences from war likely limits the range of participants we solicited for the project. These were all likely individuals who had thought more deeply about their experiences and wanted a platform to articulate their lived experience.

## INTRODUCTION TO MILITARY CULTURE FROM PAST TO PRESENT

The majority of this book focuses on veterans of the wars in Iraq and Afghanistan alone. It is comprised of firsthand accounts of military life from training to reintegrating post-deployment from these wards alongside our in-depth analysis of these accounts. As the forthcoming pages reveal, we found that there are indeed great cultural discrepancies that likely contribute to the high numbers of PTSD and suicidality in U.S. veterans. Much of this seemed to center in the divide between military and civilian cultures. It seems irresponsible to jump into these current wars without first drawing a bridge between the past and the present. If the abyss between military and civilian culture is indeed at the center of this epidemic, it is worth providing a brief overview of how that abyss was formed. In this introduction, we will sketch out the history of the military/civilian divide in the United States, as well as explore the implications of that history as they relate to our research. We will also give a brief review of some previously established theories as well as give you a roadmap for the rest of the book.

## Military/Civilian Divide in the United States

The idea that there is a military/civilian divide in the United States is certainly not novel. Rachel Maddow's (2012) work has described the development of this divide with depth and nuance. This idea is so central to what the research revealed that it is worth briefly summarizing this history using her work.

Maddow begins by tracing the presence of the divide by describing the intent that the founders had. "The founders were on to something with their cautions about the whole military vainglory thing. *There is really nothing that approaches war's political potency*" (Maddow, 2012, p. 42, emphasis added). The belief that the founders held was that too much glorification for a national military could lead to unchecked power to generals, long overseas expeditions that might not be in the national interest, and a separate feeling of entitlement for military service versus other occupations. It is important to emphasize that before this gap existed in the United States, the deepest fear of the founders was that military service might come to be seen as separate, distinct, and above the general concept of citizenship in American society. The model of citizen as servicemember and servicemember as citizen was deeply woven into the intentions of the founders, especially in light of the backdrop of British military power.

Perhaps unsurprisingly, the divide between citizens and military became deepest in the United States during and after Vietnam. This is epitomized in President Johnson's decision not to call the Reserves and National Guard though they were clearly needed. These military branches were simply too enmeshed with civilian culture to be brought into the fray. Against the founders ideal of the citizen-soldier, American leadership began to realize that it was easier to wage war with a military that looked more like a mercenary force that was intentionally separated from civilian life, culture, and society. The widespread political unrest about the choice to enter this war drew the divide even deeper. As Maddow explains, "the American troops' disenchantment with the civilian cohort was real, but so was civilian disenchantment with the Vietnam War, and the military itself" (Maddow, 2012, p. 19).

The divide only continues to grow after Vietnam. Because of the almost singular power of the executive branch to wage war, tax cuts in wartime, and smaller and smaller percentages of U.S. citizens enlisting in the military, the idea that when there is war that the country is at war becomes obsolete. Instead, the reality is that the military is at war while the civilian population is largely unaffected—and by extension, the civilian population is largely in the dark about what it means to serve. There is almost a kind of class division here. The civilians are the protected class, the military are the protecting class. Maddow summarizes the effect of these many layers of issues as follows:

> With tax cuts in wartime, with no sense of collective national sacrifice on behalf of the war effort, with less than one percent of the American population taking up arms to fight, with US casualties politically and literally shielded from the public view, the cumulative effect was to normalize our national wartime. We've become a nation "at peace with being at war," in the words of the *New York Times* media critic David Carr. And as the country learned to be untroubled by the fact that we had troops at war, troops coming home from those wars learned to look out for themselves. . . . A 2011 Pew poll found that 84 percent of post-9/11 veterans felt the public didn't understand the problems faced by service members and their families. It also found that more than two-thirds of Americans believe that the disproportionate burden shouldered by those who have served is, "just part of being in the military." (2012, p. 246)

Ultimately, the effect of centralizing war powers and selecting from such a small percentage of a population builds this sense of social isolation and distance between American veterans and American civilians.

The *New York Times* (Phillipps & Arango, 2020) recently published an article demonstrating that an increasingly smaller number of counties across America are responsible for a growingly disproportionate amount on all enlisted servicemembers. Ultimately, only *several dozen* counties across America are increasingly responsible for providing servicemembers across the military. Furthermore, the majority of families in these increasingly smaller number of counties are themselves already military families. There is a compounding effect of growing the gap between American civilian and military culture here.

Though the economic reality of war does impact society as a whole, it is quite easy to disconnect from the source of that impact when one is not connected with military culture in any way. Economists at MIT, Gruber and Simon (2019), estimate these two wars have cost the American taxpayer approximately six trillion dollars. A part of what aids the disconnection from military life is what Hillman (2004) calls "peace mongering" that is somewhat unique to American civilian culture. Peace mongering is the attempt to eschew *any* contact or awareness of suffering, trauma, and death in one's everyday life. This tendency—ubiquitous in the lives of Americans with the socioeconomic status to afford the illusion—leads veterans to feel fundamentally disconnected from and unrelated to civilians when they return from war. This disconnection, when layered with all of the other factors mentioned above, creates an unnavigable chasm between military and civilian cultures.

It is our contention that this chasm between civilian and military culture is perhaps *the most critical factor* contributing to the isolation that veterans report when they return home after deployment, and therefore the primary source of the staggering rates of PTSD and suicide in the United States.

Though this source may seem simple, the symptoms it yields within our population in the United States are wide and varied. For example, one of the arguments we will make here is that the growing social chasm between American military and American civilian culture, combined with the increasing valorization of military service in America, has contributed to the existence of a kind of social capital that can be derived from military service. This has led to a uniquely American phenomenon known as stolen valor. Stolen valor is characterized as "civilians fibbing about military service, and veterans embellishing their records with bogus claims of battlefield medals and missions with elite units" (Mockenhaupt, 2016). This issue has been prevalent enough to warrant an act of Congress, passed in 2013, to criminalize the behavior of embellishing rank, service time, or deployment status.

The existence of this phenomenon raises two questions. First, are so many servicemembers aggrandizing their service in such a way that a law was needed to criminalize this behavior? Second, are civilians who have never served falsely creating their own veteran status? If so, what could be their motivation other than money and benefits? Mockenhaupt describing the social capital tied to twenty-first-century military service in America in this post-9/11 era:

> "The second you start talking about being a war hero, you have admiration from your fellow citizens. You're a person of value," says B. G. "Jug" Burkett, a Vietnam veteran who was the first to expose military imposters in a systematic way, and who coined the term *stolen valor.* Since the mid-1980s, he's investigated about 3,000 people, outing a city-council member, the head of a Vietnam Veterans of America chapter, and a U.S. congressman. Burkett—who courted controversy himself by questioning John Kerry's war record during his 2004 presidential bid—has also exposed hundreds of veterans who claimed disabilities from wartime service they didn't perform and civilians who invented service records to collect disability benefits. "The types of fraud are beyond comprehension," he says. (Mockenhaupt, 2017)

The idea that fuels this phenomenon is that service yields a specific kind of social capital. If this is something that civilians capitalize on, it is likely also a reason that individuals enlist in the military. In other words, what stolen valor reveals is twofold—one, that the distance between civilian and servicemember is vast, and two, that to be a servicemember is to hold a special place in society. A place that awards you with things far beyond benefits and badges of honor. The ability to return to one's society with "value" is undoubtedly a tantalizing reward for many young men and women. It is perhaps especially valuable social capital for those who did not stumble easily upon recognition and acceptance in their adolescence and early adulthood. Nevertheless, the effect of such a powerful reinforcement upon the motivational trajectory of servicemembers must be considered, especially when it comes to understanding their ability to reintegrate back into the society that was supposed to grant such heavy social capital.

## Previously Established Theories

As mentioned, a significant portion of our interviews was devoted to exploring previous theories that were already established in the literature on veteran reintegration. Some of the factors that we looked to critically examine are listed and briefly explained below, along with bibliographic references to previous research in the field.

Many veterans express that they had established strong bonds of unity and solidarity with former members of their military units. However, there is likewise a significant portion of the research suggesting that veterans might struggle to replicate this sense of unity with civilian peers, coworkers, neighbors, and even family members after reintegrating. Therefore, we wanted to examine the types of relationships that are formed in veterans' civilian lives after returning from active duty service and deployment (Creech et al., 2018; Senecal et al., 2018; Junger, 2016; Junger, 2010; Kukla, Rattray, & Saylers, 2015; Browning, 2015; Nelson Goff, Crow, Reisbig, Hamilton, 2007; Friedman, 2005; Demers, 2011; Caddick, Phoenix, & Smith, 2015; Monson, Taft, & Fredman, 2009; Bowling & Sherman, 2008; Yeager et al., 2007).

There is a long history of research devoted to the psychosocial effects of identity foreclosure on individuals who are making career transitions. Much of this research comes out of an examination of retired workers and, more specifically, retired athletes (Marcia, 1966; Petitpas, 1978; Brewer et al., 1993; Petitpas & France, 2010). Admittedly, a smaller portion of research is devoted to the question of veteran identity as it relates to career transition. Nevertheless, there is a growing body of research in this field that directly and indirectly explores the phenomenon of identity formation, identity foreclosure, career transition, and career adaptation with veterans (Libin et al., 2017; Lancaster, Kintzle, & Castro, 2018; Razanova et al., 2016; Brinn & Auerbach, 2015). In this project, we wanted to explore the differences between American and NATO ally veterans when it came to identity transition. In short, we believe there are grounds to argue that the experience of identity transition a veteran undergoes in one's civilian life after returning from active duty service and deployment will have a significant effect on his or her ability to move into civilian life.

We wanted to examine the specific deployment transition programs, civilian reintegration programs, and therapeutic programs offered across different cultures and what effect these have had on the return to civilian life.

Specifically, we are concerned with the unwavering commitment to time-sensitive and short-term-focused interventions offered to servicemembers. Certainly, the American military and American medical culture both rely on swiftness and effectiveness regarding intervention into "problems." There can be a consistent gravitational pull in these cultures to reduce ambiguity and uncertainty into clear, effective, and efficient solutions. We wanted to examine whether these same principles are at play in NATO ally nations. If the reintegration processes were indeed different (e.g., if they offered more time), we wanted to see what effect that might have had on transitions out of active duty.

A critical examination of the training process of both American and NATO ally servicemembers was performed. Specifically, we wanted to look deeply at the formation of idealism, military ideology, identity formation, and specific norms of masculinity in these respective military cultures. By idealism, we mean the cognitive formation of perfectionism and excessive conscientiousness as is formed in American servicemembers immediately in initial entry training environments (Senecal & McDonald, 2018). By military ideology, we will discuss the forms of operant and classical conditioning used to promote hero worship and kill rates in American servicemembers over the last century (Grossman, 1995). Finally, we became interested in the type of identity, specifically as it relates to masculine identity in combat MOS jobs, that was promoted and conditioned into servicemembers through their initial entry training processes. We suspected that this type of identity could have a significant effect on the ability to return to civilian life and civilian relationships after active duty (Gallagher, 2016).

We wanted to examine the social safety nets in NATO ally countries versus in America and how these did or did not impact the effect of transition to civilian life. Specifically, the tenants of self-reliance, consumerism, and capitalism must be given serious examination when considering the ramifications of our nation's veterans. Capitalism relies on functioning and producing bodies. There are unique nuances germane to the American reintegration process that tacitly support this tendency to promote the productivity and effectiveness of the servicemember as quickly as possible when he or she reenters civilian life.

How willing civilians in NATO allies are to engage in the details of the lives of military servicemembers in that nation. Hillman (2004) describes how consumerism relies on a principle he terms as "peace mongering." In short, in order to continue as consumers first, serious systemic efforts must be made to deter American society from any critical analysis or serious reflection on the complexity of human existence, in particular, of those associated with human suffering and death. We suggest that the tendency of veterans and civilians to have a shared experience and empathy in the suffering of war is likely to aid their transition into civilian life after active duty service and deployment.

Ultimately, we were looking to hypothesize that there are scientific and theoretical grounds to posit that, when it comes to conceptualizing mental illness in American veterans, the phenomenon is severely more complicated and sociocultural than it is often presented. By complicated, we mean specifically that there are profound sociocultural elements that are being overlooked in the conceptualization process of PTSD and complex PTSD in American veterans from Operation Enduring Freedom (OEF) and Operation Iraqi Freedom (OIF). Thus, any tendencies to reduce the reintegration difficulties for veterans work against understanding and recovery. In general, there is a tendency to medicalize all mental illness in American culture. The tendency to undergo a reductionist conceptualization of mental illness, the mind, and the social/emotional dimensions of human experience is playing a role in limiting access to a more holistic and, consequently, more effective form of treatment for veterans who experience reintegration difficulties or symptoms related to PTSD. Our goal is to use this research project to push back against this tendency and paint a more sociocultural mosaic of the phenomenon.

## New Directions and Current Themes

In many ways, this book is just the beginning of this investigation. A complete causal account of PTSD in America is simply beyond the scope of this work. In fact, the data contained so many relevant threads and supporting evidence that much of it had to be bracketed out for future work. This is not to say that progress cannot be made, of course. The data that we gathered is telling, and it sketches a grim narrative. Most broadly, we identify two general areas that prime servicemembers for and then reinforce the lasting and intractable presence of PTSD. These areas are the military training process and the social dimensions of the reintegration process post-deployment and/or after active duty. We believe that aspects of these phenomena are unique in the United States in ways that make it more likely for servicemembers to develop PTSD, and more difficult to heal from it. In this book, we will unpack four critical factors that we believe lead to the development and lasting nature of PTSD in America after the wars in Iraq and Afghanistan.

The first factor that our research showed is that the problems that arise with reintegration likely begin before deployment, specifically, when America trains servicemembers to go to war. We found that there is an implicit ideology surrounding training the military in America is steeped in perfectionism, idealism, and hero worship in a way that erodes personal identity before the servicemember even deploys. Not only is this something that American servicemembers report as being corrosive, it is also something that is missing from the training methods and ideologies of our NATO allies.

The second factor finds its roots in the training process and later manifests itself in active duty lifestyle and deployment setting. Here, we will focus on the concept of identity that is promoted and reinforced in many military communities in America. Furthermore, we will attempt to differentiate this form of American military identity from the forms of military identity that are more likely to manifest in NATO allies. Ultimately, we will argue that once adopted, this form of identity makes it difficult, if not impossible, for American veterans and servicemembers to form strong relationships with civilian counterparts.

The third factor has to do with the interpersonal support system that the servicemember has upon one's return. In both our previous research (Senecal et al., 2018) and in this current project, we found that the support network that servicemembers had in place made an enormous difference in the success of their reintegration. We found other cultures to be far superior when it came to providing the kinds of relationship support necessary to servicemembers upon return from war. This is worth noting not simply because it highlights an area where we are failing in America, but also because it provides the beginning details from which we can build a new blueprint for supporting servicemembers as they reintegrate into civilian society post-military career. This includes an analysis of the programs that have been put in place in America to help servicemembers and their families through the training, deployment, and reintegration processes. There is a commitment in America to short-term, universalized, focused interventions—despite the fact that they regularly lack effectiveness. It is worth noting here that the acknowledgment that servicemembers struggle upon their return is relatively new. While it is encouraging that these programs exist, they are not comprehensive enough to capture the various ways that veterans struggle once they arrive home. In addition, they cease at six months post-deployment, and then can completely miss servicemembers who do not develop PTSD symptoms right away.

The fourth and final factor uncovered in our research was perhaps the most unique and most unexpected at the outset of our work. Though we did hypothesize about the effects of idealism on American veterans, we did not anticipate how this mindset might lead to self-aggrandizing tendencies and entitlement among Americans. Furthermore, we did not anticipate just how rare these tendencies would be in NATO ally veterans. We will speak more specifically about these factors in the final chapter of the analysis; however, it is important to note the intersecting relationship of these factors at least briefly. In short, idealism leads servicemembers to construct some idealized version of what military service should look like and be. Because this image is an ideal, and one that is conditioned into American servicemembers in the training process, it is always impossible to obtain. In the face of this impossibility, the servicemember begins to experience a ubiquitous sense of shame and guilt for his or her failure to obtain the ideal. As is usually the case, the effects of shame are not contained to their own island. Many American participants described how this sense of shame metamorphosized into a form of self-aggrandizement, what many participants described as an insidious culture of lying and self-promotion in the American military. This also had effects on the perception of military identity veterans clung to after service (Eichler, 2017), as well as perceptions of service formed toward other servicemembers, especially in regard to diminishing the service of other veterans (Gallagher, 2016). This tendency to self-aggrandize and distort one's service record—at times coined as "stolen valor"—then leads to a form of entitlement for oneself and, consequently, disdain for civilians who did not serve.

As we unpack each of these factors, using the qualitative data that we gathered in our interviews, we are making an argument about the very nature of PTSD as an illness. In short, we are arguing that if there is an "illness" to be addressed regarding veteran reintegration, it exists in the lifeblood of the sociocultural factors salient to a society and not solely in the mind or body of veterans. We are suggesting that the society they come from and return to will have a profound impact on the journey home.

The signature wounds left by the Iraq and Afghanistan wars have proven to be lasting and devastating. They must be borne by us all, not just by our servicemembers. We hope that this work sketches the outlines of the problem, and that future work can help us fully address it so that our military and civilian cultures can become healthier and more in tune with one another.

## *Chapter 1*

# Planting the Seeds for PTSD in Military Training

### THE ROOTS OF TRAUMA IN TRAINING

In the study of combat trauma, it is perhaps unsurprising that the focus has been on the experiences at war and the conditions upon returning home and not at all on the training process. As we began to draw the arc back to find the roots of the problem, however, we discovered that traumatic experience could actually begin as early as basic training. The way that a servicemember is prepared for war, and the circumstances under which that preparation takes place, can potentially have a great impact on both the experience of combat and the ease (or lack of ease) upon returning home.

We isolated four areas within training that were potentially problematic: toxic training dynamics that can lead to a breakdown of identity, the reinforcement of a split between military and civilian lives in which military lives are seen as superior, hero worship, and other forms of destructive idealism, and unrealistic expectations of combat which often go unmet.

What was perhaps most striking—other than these threads which appeared in almost every American interview that we completed—was the complete lack of these experiences in interviewees from other cultures. There were times when we would ask questions based on training methods in America that Israeli or German servicemembers simply could not understand. In cultures that had similar training programs (e.g., Canada and Britain), there were accordingly higher rates of PTSD and suicide when compared to cultures that did not. To be sure, more work needs to be done here in order to make a causal connection. However, our qualitative data showed significantly relevant trends that are worth noting. Before considering the phenomenological experience of training, it is helpful to lay out a roadmap for what training looks like across the cultures that we looked at (American,

Canadian, British, Israeli, and Norwegian), as well as how much time is spent in combat.

## MILITARY TRAINING AND TIME IN THEATER

### American

The majority of the American participants in this study were enlisted servicemembers from the Army. The average amount of time it takes to train an enlisted American servicemember is, roughly, one week of in-processing, ten weeks of basic training, and a final advanced individual training (AIT) relative to that servicemember's military occupation specialty (MOS). Training in some of these MOS schools can be as short as five weeks (e.g., infantry), with others lasting as long as more than a year (e.g., patriot system repairs or special operations).

Something that is shared across branches of the military is a complete divorce from civilian society for the duration of training. Basic training involves no time off base, little to no cell-phone and internet usage, and no civilian visitors (until a 48-hour pass is issued at graduation). AIT will involve cell-phone access but little to no off-base passes during the workweek and perhaps even for the first few weeks of AIT. Furthermore, many American military bases are themselves physically removed from American military culture. They contain almost all of the amenities on-base that an individual would need and want (grocery stores, PX's, gyms, theaters, restaurants, and even water parks).

Of all the branches of the American military, the training process for the Marines is the most extreme. Marine recruits are taken to Paris Island, a 5,000-person county located off the southeast coast of South Carolina. Initial entry training is roughly thirteen weeks for basic training, another five weeks for infantry training (all Marines have to be trained for infantry, regardless of MOS), and then Marines will enter AIT for their respective MOS. During this time, the use of cell phones, internet access, and civilian contact and communication are severely limited, if not completely cut off.

When it comes to time spent in theater on deployments, this differs depending on the branch of the military. Army soldiers were required to spend the most time in theater on deployments. During the surges in Iraq and Afghanistan, average deployments for Army veterans were fifteen months in theater. Outside of the surge, average Army deployments range from nine to twelve months in duration. U.S. Marine deployments are consistently six months in length, while Air Force and Navy deployments are, respectively, between four and six months and six and nine months (Institute of Medicine, 2013).

It is worth noting that American participants reported the most extensive and severe exposure to combat while in theater. This sentiment was often corroborated by NATO allies, as well, with NATO participants often saying that their American peers were regularly exposed to heavier combat exposure and more dangerous missions. Overall, there was a sentiment expressed by both American and NATO allies that American officers were far less likely to scale back the mission regardless of the risks and adversity posed to servicemembers. On the other hand, American and NATO allies often acknowledged that the NATO ally mission was pursued with far more caution and prudence.

## Canadian

The Canadian training process is very similar to the American process. It is roughly the same length of time as U.S. Army training and often occurs on military bases that are relatively removed from civilian life. Civilian contact is severely limited during this time period for Canadian recruits and there are similar basic restrictions to cell-phone usage and civilian contact. It would be fair to say that Canadians have a very similar training process to U.S. Army veterans. Finally, Canadian servicemembers spend an average of seven to eight months on deployment.

## British

The British training process is also quite similar to the Canadian and American training process. The length of initial entry training is shorter, but personal freedoms such as cell-phone usage and internet access are similarly restricted. The major difference between the Canadian and American training process is the proximity to civilian life and access to civilian contact, communication, and lifestyles. While the British military intend to build restrictions around civilian contact into their training process, the geography of England makes it far more difficult to isolate recruits from civilian contact. Many of the British veterans in this study described how they were always within a relatively short drive from their family through their training and service requirements on active duty. Finally, British servicemembers spend between six and eight months on deployment.

## German

The German training process is radically different from that of the American, Canadian, or British experience. After World War II, the German military made a focused and concerted effort to ensure that the military would never again be in a position of autocratic and political manipulation moving forward. The intention was to create a citizen-soldier rather than a soldier separate from civilians. Much of this was modeled after an early-American model of the National Guard and a form of service that never divorces the servicemember's training and duties from his or her responsibilities to citizenship and higher virtues of peace and democracy.

German servicemembers are allowed to go home on weekends during initial entry training and they have cell-phone and internet access in the evenings after the training day is complete. It is worth noting that this is an intentional training methodology established by the German military to perform the exact opposite function of the American training ideology.

While Americans (as well as Canadians and the British) place deep value on the distance the military could get from civilian life and culture in order to reform the social cognition of the recruit in initial entry training. Germans see this distance as potentially dangerous to the psyche of a military recruit. Fully removing a recruit from civilian life and indoctrinating him/her with military culture would serve in only building a univocal and unyielding sense of identity in the servicemember. Though this could be useful in the short term, because of the past the German military feared the long-term effects of any conditioning process that occurs alongside civilian isolation. Finally, German servicemembers spend between four and six months on deployment.

## Israeli

The Israeli training process is also different from the cultures examined here. To begin with, Israel has mandatory conscription. This makes a separation between civilians and servicemembers impossible. There is no need to train Israeli servicemembers in isolation from Israeli civilians because Israeli civilians are *all* tied to the Israeli military through their own experiences of service.

Similar to German servicemembers, members of Israeli military are in regular contact with their friends and family throughout initial entry training and are often able to go home on the weekends to spend time with their families while on active duty. Secondly, similar to Britain, the geography of Israel is such that Israeli servicemembers, regardless of where they are stationed, will never be more than a relatively short drive away from their friends, family, and civilian home. Israeli participants often repeated that there was no sense of distance from civilians—even when returning from active service because no matter whom they encountered, they shared a similar background and service.

Israeli deployments are quite short; servicemembers spent a few weeks to months deployed on short missions. Israelis experienced just as much combat exposure as Americans in theater; however, the Israeli mission is typically shorter in duration despite the high intensity of enemy contact.

### Norwegian

The military training process in Norway is similar to that of Germany. It is shorter than American, Canadian, and British training, and involves much more civilian contact. Norwegian deployments last between four and six months. Both German and Norwegian participants reported that though there was undoubtedly combat exposure for these NATO allies and several were in fire fights with Al-Qaeda, the combat mission and combat maneuvers were far more conservative in their fighting with the enemy. These participants often expressed how American partners in theater were far more likely to be put in riskier scenarios when fighting the enemy.

Now that we have some understanding of the ways that training circumstances and deployment lengths compare, we can delve into the four ways that American servicemembers are primed for trauma before they deploy. We will look at these each in turn. Since we are isolating ways in which American servicemembers are primed for trauma and our NATO allies are not, the discussion here is mostly limited to the American experience with occasional reference to that of our NATO allies. What was most noteworthy is something that cannot be noted except to say that while these threads were persistent in each of the interviews with American servicemembers, they were nonexistent in interviews with others.

## TOXIC TRAINING DYNAMICS—IDENTITY BREAKDOWN

The idea that the American military training culture involves potentially toxic psychosocial elements is not new. There have been books and movies devoted to this idea (and exaggerations of it) in popular culture since the 1950s. What we found, however, was more subtle and nuanced than the idea that one could be negatively impacted by brutal leadership and scare tactics in training.

There were two main threads that came up continuously: infantilization and/or a dysfunctional and codependent family dynamic between leadership and cadets; and an isolating and rigid structure that completely takes over agency and connection to the outside world (indeed, noteworthy is that it creates a division between the inside and the outside world at all), which then completely falls away post-deployment. This can leave servicemembers isolated and without structure.

Many participants talked about dysfunction in the structure of the relationships with leadership. Participants often noted that it is understood that the military structure is supposed to replace their civilian support group entirely. This happens by force and also by circumstance. American military bases are contained areas that just happen to geographically isolate servicemembers from civilians. Servicemembers also consistently reported that they were forcibly isolated from connection with civilians, that their leaders became "mom and dad," and that all decision-making agency (even in off-time) was stripped away in training. Rather than learn to take care of themselves and being given the agency to make their own decisions, cadets are encouraged within this dynamic to regress as their leaders take on the role of parent and they take on the role of a child. They act out and leave their behavior up to the interpretation and action of their leaders. As American #7 explained:

> Leadership though, it's family. The first sergeant is your mom, the commander is your dad. They both do different roles. You expect your parents to be paying attention all the time if your kid comes home from school and he smells like weed, or he looks fucked up or he's lethargic. . . . As military leaders, you are supposed to be paying attention to this stuff all the time. It's when leaders don't that people slip through the cracks that it fosters that toxic growth.

This odd and potentially dysfunctional relationship seems counter to the strength and independence that are upheld as primary values in all branches of the military. Cadets are children in this structure, and they learn that they are not solely responsible for their behavior; it is also up to the scrutiny and action of their leaders. This also puts an unnecessary amount of pressure on leaders to care for the mental health and wellness of their cadets in addition to their military training and education.

This familial bond is solidified by the fact that cadets are also completely isolated from their home support networks for various lengths of time, even when they have time off. American #4 summarizes his experience of initial entry training as an Army soldier:

> Civilian contact is just not a thing . . . for the first ten weeks, you're confined to base. You don't get to go. Your weekends are spent sorting out your gear and going to the gym and being marched to the kitchen.

While cadets in other cultures had a reasonable amount of time off and could socialize with civilians in their off-time, this is not an option for American cadets. This imposed structure which bleeds into the little free time that cadets have leaves them totally constrained—in a way that is entirely unmatched in civilian life. This not only leads to isolation in training but strengthens the divide between military and civilian culture that we mentioned in the introduction. This intense family dynamic is something that veterans often report missing when they reenter civilian life.

These dynamics—though they are *not* replicated across cultures—are assumed by Americans to be necessary. Prevalent is the idea that if things were different, cadets would not be trained as well, loyalty would not be as strong, and that general effectiveness would suffer. Controlling and isolating tactics—which break down self-identity and also resilience—are seen as methods of making sure that cadets are "really ready" for deployment, and that loyalty is not a question when they serve. American #8 summarizes what many said:

> They took your phone and you weren't allowed to speak to your family. They really made it tough because *they want to weed out the weak ones that get homesick and what not.*

There is an underlying toxic idea here, which is that if a cadet misses home or needs civilian contact, they are *too weak* to go to war. This unnecessarily extreme isolation from the civilian world creates a situation where cadets have to "prove" that they have more or less conquered their own emotions, that they do not need to be connected to society outside of the military, and that they have welcomed military identity in place of personal identity. They are celebrated for *not* feeling, for *not* needing to be connected to social networks at home, and for being able to get everything that they need from their fellow cadets and their leaders.

American #13 expresses the arc of isolation and how it feeds into the familial bonds of combat:

> After spending so long away from home I just lost touch with a lot of different people. And don't get me wrong you make friends along the way but the people that you bled the fight with, that's your real family. It's hard to replace them.

This is a sentiment we saw repeated often—that the bonds that you create with military members are meant to replace the ones you had before, that this family is to become your "real" family. What we should notice here is that there are already two ways in which reintegration becomes difficult before the servicemember has even deployed. First, the civilian support structure is entirely replaced. Second, the cadet is taught to stop wanting that civilian connection. Put another way, we train our servicemembers to become disconnected from the civilian world when they join the military, to stop even desiring a connection with the civilian world, and then we wonder why they feel disconnected when they come home. The fundamental disconnect between military members and civilians makes reintegration more difficult.

This kind of mentality was largely missing among NATO allies. It is also worth noting that *all of this* runs counter to resilience training, which focuses on fostering a strong sense of self, a broad set of social connections, and rich self-awareness.

## US VERSUS THEM: PROBLEMATIC MILITARY/ CIVILIAN HIERARCHY IN TRAINING

American veterans almost unequivocally reported that they felt superior to civilians during and after they completed training. Again, the creation of this power dynamic is assumed to be a necessary part of the military training complex, as it is widely believed that servicemembers need to see civilians as inferior in order to understand them as a population that needs protection. While this is thought to increase motivation, it has the perhaps unintentional effect of planting the seeds for a toxic power dynamic. This dynamic reinforces the idea that servicemembers are doing work that civilians cannot do, but that needs to be done, which can also foster a sense of resentment toward civilians.

As American #1 reported, this sense of feeling responsible for protecting civilians who could not or would not protect themselves worked to fortify this sentiment:

> American civilians were viewed as people we were supposed to protect . . . and the vast majority of them are not going to defend themselves so we have to do the work for them.

Initial entry recruits are taught from the very beginning of training that there is a strict divide between servicemembers and civilians. Servicemembers protect; civilians are protected. They don't understand us; we don't understand them. We do what they don't want to, so they don't have to. This creates a power dynamic that provides a rich breeding ground for resentment and rage—not just simple disconnection.

American MV reported that it was part of the Reserve Officer Training Cadet (ROTC) culture in college to talk negatively about fellow students who were not ROTC:

> We had no right to be like that because we had really done nothing, we are just cadets. But we talk about civilians like we hate them and they piss us off. When we get up for PT at 5 am and we go to our eight am class after and there's some

sorority girl complaining that the walk to class was cold and she was up too early, we are all like "fuck this person, we've been up since five and we were working out in this shit weather."

As we can see here, work in training is viewed as fundamentally different from *any* work done in the civilian world—the work in training is harder, and it cannot be understood or imagined by the civilian. This creates a toxic "us vs. them" dynamic that is scaffolded not just by difference but by hatred. As we see in this servicemember's reporting, it is not just that civilians are different; they are less.

This disconnect between civilian and servicemember is further reinforced as cadets are constantly reminded during training that very few serve in the military, and that it is exceptionally rare to even make it through training. While the goal here may be to foster self-esteem, veterans frequently reported that they felt "untouchable" and superior to civilians in a way that contributed to their disconnection with the civilian world.

When asked about whether he felt disconnected from civilians during training, Canadian #3 explained:

It's in a formative part of your career that they turn you into an overconfident zealot and that's what you need to be for your job. You feel like that's part of your career and it eventually settles. I mean reality sets in but during training, they're trying to deprogram someone and reprogram them into being able to do some pretty horrific shit so yes, the contact with civilians totally broke in battle school, for sure. I wouldn't say (I felt) detachment so much as a misplaced sense of superiority.

Again, we see the belief that this kind of programming and disconnection is necessary alongside the recognition that it is harmful. In the very same sentence that this servicemember says that training turned him into an "overconfident zealot," he says that this is necessary in order to be able to do his job. Not that it helped, or enhanced his work, but that it was *necessary*.

In the UK, Norway, and Germany, this kind of separation is simply not present. Initial entry servicemembers are allowed to contact their family, have access to their phones at night, and even often go home on the weekends. Geographically, they are enmeshed in civilian culture and not physically separated. Perhaps unsurprisingly, they did not report having this sense of disconnection or of superiority over their civilian counterparts.

While this sense of disconnection and superiority begins in training for many, it causes serious problems when veterans return from training and/or deployment and find that they cannot connect with civilians anymore in the way that they did before. American #6 describes this sentiment:

> Nevertheless, when I first got back, I was really disconnected, I couldn't establish a connection with really anyone at the time other than other army guys. I found when I was at school, I met quite a few veterans that were in school, those were the only guys and girls I was able to connect too. I felt like I couldn't connect with anyone in the world except these types of people.

The moment that training begins, the world is strictly divided into military and civilian camps and when veterans attempt to reintegrate post-deployment, they no longer belong to either camp. They haven't been civilians since before training, and they are no longer servicemembers either. They are only veterans, and so they come to believe that they can only connect to other veterans.

Not only are cadets encouraged to hold themselves above civilians in training, they are also encouraged to hold themselves to unrealistic expectations—model themselves after mythical war heroes. This impossible idealism and hero worship also contribute to the fragmentation of identity that makes it so hard to come home and recognize oneself.

## HERO WORSHIP—SETTING IMPOSSIBLE GOALS

The American war hero is an archetype that spans the military–civilian divide. It is upheld most fervently during training across branches of the military. Each branch has its own exemplars of the ideal servicemember and these are thought to serve an integral purpose in the training process. They are held up as a unifying goal—each servicemember is to strive to be as close to that ideal as possible. Pointed examples of courage, valor, and flawless performance are constantly upheld to servicemembers as they train so that they have something to aim for.

The problem with this is that these examples are typically taken from wars long past and representative of styles of battle that simply no longer exist. These exemplars are then *impossible* to replicate in modern war, and this often leads to guilt and failure when servicemembers do not—and cannot—live up to the ideal set for them in training. Marine #3, former infantry Marine, explains this sentiment:

> You get into boot camp there is absolute hero worship. You learn to memorize Carlos Hathcock and Dan Dailey and Smedly Butler and the two-time Medal of Honor winners. You memorize that and you worship these people. You are conditioned to worship these people because these people went out and in the process of completing those two things in very extraordinary circumstances and you worship those people. Trying to become those guys is like being a football

> player and saying you are going to be Tom Brady. It is never going to happen. The chances of you being in that situation where you could prove yourself in that manner are so infinitesimal it is mind blowing. But until you have been pinned with that medal, until you've pulled that shit off, you feel like a failure.

Carlos Hathcock was a Marine sniper who had 93 confirmed kills during Vietnam. These are only the *confirmed* killed; Hathcock is estimated to have killed between 300 and 400 enemies during the Vietnam War. So unprecedented was this number that there is a rifle named after Hathcock. Smedley Butler was the most decorated war hero in history at the time of his death in 1940. By the end of his career with the Marines, he had received sixteen medals of honor. He received the Medal of Honor twice, and he is the only Marine to have been awarded the Brevet Medal and two Medals of Honor—all for separate instances. It is worth noting that the most recent war that these two heralded war heroes fought in was Vietnam. This participant compares trying to become these guys with being a football player and trying to become Tom Brady. We would argue that it is actually much more difficult to achieve this hero status when war has changed so drastically.

This hero worship in boot camp is thought to serve a motivating purpose. The idea is that this gives servicemembers a tangible goal to aim for, which will enhance their behavior in combat. Servicemembers that hear these stories and hold onto them in combat situations are more likely to act "heroically" in order to live up to those expectations that are set for them by the military, and that they in turn set for themselves. The problem is that there is no way to meet those expectations, and even more problematically, there is no method for helping veterans cope with that failure.

The ideal solider is a paradigm that is so pervasive that it is one of the reasons that servicemembers will often embellish their war stories so that their experience more closely matches that of the ideals they model themselves after. There is a pervasive and singular idea of what war should look like, and what kinds of experiences a hero has, and when the theater of war doesn't offer this, the servicemember has to compensate for it by lying or exaggerating their experience. An American participant explains:

> When you start talking about the embellishments, like why guys lie, good or bad, nobody wants to admit it, but everyone does it. You embellish the story so you can convey some extreme level of emotion that you felt in that moment and the only way you can ensure somebody else reacts that same way is to make the story so outlandish. That is why so many guys exaggerate about other people's exploits or their own.

What war *feels* like might be the same—one feels terror, danger, extreme stress—but what war *looks* like is radically different, and therefore the narratives no longer fit. The societal narrative about war does not match what war is like. One has to exaggerate in order to be understood. This leads to a vicious cycle of shame in which the servicemember gets accolades and positive attention from civilians, but they know that it comes as a result of lying and exaggerating their experience. They get what they need—but they also know that they got it because they lied. This isolating discord reinforces the core fear that the individual *did* fail as a solider.

This idealism does not remain contained within the realm of what the servicemember should *be* like; it bleeds into what combat should *look* like. When the expectations of combat differ radically from the experience of combat, the servicemember has a hard time placing himself and his experience into the societal narrative about war and trauma. Certain things come to be understood as heroic, traumatic, or even simply paradigmatic of combat. This is problematic for two reasons. First, it ignores the firsthand experience of the servicemembers—who then do not get much say about what it was actually like for them. Second, we set the servicemembers up for failure from the outset when we arm them with an expectation of war that goes unmet. Both these elements provide a fertile ground for trauma—before the servicemember even deploys.

## UNMET EXPECTATIONS OF COMBAT

The idealism and hero worship discussed in the previous section tie in with the idea that servicemembers often go to war with expectations of combat simply go unmet. This causes problems in two ways. The first is that when we have these outdated conceptions of what combat is like, this contributes to civilian misunderstanding of what is traumatic about war. The second is that we set servicemembers up for failure and disappointment when we set expectations of combat that are impossible to meet because the very nature of combat has changed. On the civilian side, this leads to a fragmented understanding of the roots of PTSD and misunderstandings of what kinds of experience can be traumatic. On the military side, it leads to a problematically unsatisfying experience of war.

The former issue is epitomized in the case of Bowe Bergdahl, an American Army soldier, who deserted his post in 2009 and was subsequently captured and held by the Taliban for five years. Though the circumstances of his desertion have been debated since, Bergdahl himself admitted to his family and to the media that he left his post because he was disappointed with the deployment. He did not feel that the experience of combat matched the expectations that were set up in training.

Armed with the idealism described in the section above and hoping for an exciting combat experience in which he could prove his heroism, Bergdahl ended up serving in a deployment that failed to meet his expectations. In turn, this did not give him the opportunity to prove what a hero he was. In his own words:

> I had this fantastic idea that I was going to prove to the world that, you know, I was the real thing. You know, I could be, you know, what . . . I could be what it is that every . . . you know, all those guys out there who go to the movies and watch those movies, they all want to be that. But I wanted to prove that I was that. (Bergdahl, 2016)

Here we see that for Bergdahl, the ideals of war were present before he even went to training—they were the very reason he joined the Army in the first place. Bergdahl's deployment took place on a base in Afghanistan, and it was not a glamorous one. Tasked with monitoring the area for improvised explosive devices, Bergdahl's battalion was in a long and boring mission that felt meaningless and poorly led. Frustrated at leadership, and the fact that his complaints seemed to be falling on deaf ears, he decided to take matters into his own hands and leave the forward operating base. He said that his hope was that a call would go out when he was found to be missing and that his complaints would then finally reach the ears of higher-ups who could change the course of the mission. What he hadn't planned on was getting kidnapped by the Taliban. The search for Bergdahl required significant resources from the Army and several members of his battalion lost their lives searching for him. Five years after his capture, Bergdahl was released as a part of a prisoner exchange for five Taliban members that were being held at Guantanamo Bay. Bergdahl was court-martialed and eventually dishonorably discharged from the Army. Though this is only one case, it is still indicative of the underlying problem—the vision of war that we are selling to cadets simply does not match the modern realities of war.

Indeed, outdated ideals of combat are still presented to servicemembers throughout their military careers. In an article about leadership style, a former U.S. Army infantry officer writes about what he calls "sledgehammer style":

> With the light infantry company—men, mostly in their early twenties—my style was to inspire and pump them up like a high school football team. They were tough young infantry servicemembers and needed a charismatic leader. During company runs—I would be out in front of the formation literally running with a sledgehammer. "The guys loved it. Kind of like Patton's approach with his ivory handled pistols." (Smith, 2007)

General Patton is not just a war hero; he has become a sort of mythological creature. His audacious ivory-handled pistols (worth noting that he carried two, not just one) were used to perform unprecedented tasks of combat—killing the combatant and his horse at the same time, for example. Moreover, they were also known to inspire his troops. Those pearl-handled pistols were symbols—symbols of superhuman fearlessness, of superhuman strength. "We shall attack and attack until we are exhausted, and then we shall attack again," he was known to say.

The problem with ideals that are based in methods of combat that are no longer relevant is that it leads to the following tensions and questions. What can be done when this is the style in which you are trained, and then when you actually deploy there is no hand-to-hand combat at all? Are you still a war hero? How can you be sure? What kind of story can you tell about it when you get home? How can you get people to understand the importance of a mission when you cannot find the importance yourself?

Bergdahl's case could perhaps be dismissed if we bracket out those who see combat from those who do not. One might be tempted to say that this kind of dissatisfaction with war is only a risk with people who are placed on missions that are necessary but feel worthless. However, even when servicemembers are engaged in direct combat, what combat looks like is still drastically different from what it used to be. We've come a long way from Patton's ivory pistols and the sledgehammer. And these technological advancements are arguably necessary for certain combat missions. Where we once had Carlos Hathcock and his 400 sniper kills in Vietnam, we now have drone pilots who fly their drones from safe, offsite locations.

As mentioned previously, there are large numbers of veterans who are being diagnosed with PTSD who have not spent much time on the front lines or even seen combat. How can this be? If what is traumatic about war is the terror one feels when one's life is in grave danger for months at a time, how can it be possible to be traumatized when one's life has not been in grave danger at all? Again, we are met with the idea that the source of trauma is more complex than previously thought. As the contours of war change, we have to continue to revise our understanding of war and the trauma that follows.

One stark example that reveals how little we have revised our understanding of war and trauma is this use of drone technology. The military has been using unmanned aerial vehicles, more typically referred to as drones, since 2014. Their entrance into warfare was swift; in OIF and OEF alone, drones flew over 1,00,000 flight hours. Sometimes they are used to simply collect data—flying over large swaths of land and taking photos and videos. Other times, they have a much more active role and are used to kill what are called "high-value targets" from the sky.

There are two relevant things to note about the use of this technology. First, drone pilots quit in unprecedented numbers. Second, engaging in drone combat seems to be creating a *new* kind of combat trauma, appropriately termed "drone trauma." A differentiating feature of drone trauma is the incredibly unsettling *ease* with which the job is done. Servicemembers report:

> It was horrifying to know how easy it was. I felt like a coward because I was halfway around the world and the guy never even knew I was there. I felt like I was haunted by a legion of the dead. My physical health was gone, my mental health crumbled. . . . When you are exposed to it over and over again it becomes like a small video, embedded in your head, forever on repeat, causing psychological pain and suffering that many people will hopefully never experience. (Chaterjee, 2015)

There is intense stigma even within the military when it comes to being a drone pilot. This technology directly contradicts traditional concepts of war and combat, which stipulate that an essential part of being in combat is having an experience that puts the body of the solider in grave danger. The trauma of the drone combatant is even more stigmatized than the trauma of the combat servicemember. The question is phrased like this: How dare you claim to be traumatized when your life was not even in danger the way that mine was?

Regardless of what age of technology we are in, the archetype of the traumatized veteran in popular culture has us imagine a stoic character that participates in real—not virtual—violence with strength and purpose, and then later on becomes tragically haunted by the experience of it. What we see with drone technology is that it might be the *method* of killing that changes the way one feels about the killing. If it feels too easy, one may be more likely to feel guilty. Why does it feel too easy? Because drone use is not built into our typical expectations of combat—which are stuck in General Patton's time.

All of this is to say that the conceptions of war that the servicemember is armed with upon deployment are bound to shape his experience in one way or another. It would serve us to be more careful with the expectations of combat that we are setting up, as it seems we may inadvertently be setting servicemembers up for failure. When we don't adjust our training modules to the realities of war, we project false narratives about what combat is like for both servicemembers and citizens, making reintegration unnecessarily difficult in a number of ways.

## CONCLUSION

One of the things that surprised us in our research was that the roots of PTSD didn't always appear where we thought they would. They did not always spring up from these moments of battlefield trauma that we so often associate with PTSD. Sometimes, it seemed that the roots of PTSD could be found all the way back in the training process—long before the servicemember left for combat at all.

When we set out to figure out why, our central question was this: what is it about training that begins to set the servicemember up for isolation, shame, and potentially PTSD? What we found is that the roots of PTSD can be uncovered by examining the complex relationships that begin in the training process.

Though there are likely additional ways in which servicemembers are primed for trauma when they begin training, we isolated four areas in this study. The first was the toxic dynamic that often exists during basic training. This dynamic leads to a stunting and/or breakdown of identity that makes it difficult to recognize oneself. The second was the creation and reinforcement of a divide between the military and civilian worlds—both geographically and hierarchically. Instilling a belief system in the servicemember that he is doing what the civilian cannot and will not do breeds feelings of superiority, resentment, and even, in extreme cases, loathing between military and civilians—inevitably making the reintegration process painful even if one does not deploy. The third was the hero worship and idealism that are meant to motivate servicemembers in training, but often set them up to feel as if they failed even if they did not. Finally, there was the unrealistic expectations of combat that lead to deep misunderstanding of what both combat and combat trauma are like both within and outside of the military.

While this is perhaps just a gloss on the many ways that being an American servicemember is difficult in ways that are not present in our NATO allies, it is worth emphasizing the point that what makes combat traumatic, and what makes reintegration difficult, is not simply combat itself, but the training process that leads up to it. The dynamics and power structures inherent in the training process can begin to splinter the identity of the servicemember in ways that are only reified as he deploys.

*Chapter 2*

# Identity

We hypothesized at the outset of this study that the way veterans conceptualized their sense of military identity would have a significant effect on their ability to transition well into life after active duty service. Consistent with the literature, we found that veterans who were able to *diversify* their sense of identity and build a sense of self-complexity beyond the military reported greater life satisfaction upon reintegration. Perhaps unsurprisingly, the reverse was also true. Many participants, both American and NATO allies, expressed that the biggest barrier in the way of successful reintegration was the inability to move beyond a univocal commitment to military identity.

This struggle was far more prevalent in American veterans than it was in our NATO allies. In fact, when NATO ally veterans discussed this difficulty, they self-reported two striking things. The first was that though they recognized this barrier in other veterans, they did not experience it themselves. The second was that they all noticed that it was their American counterparts that seemed to struggle the most. In other words, whereas American veterans had tremendous difficulty reconciling their military identity with their life post-service, NATO ally veterans reported that this shift was much smoother for them. That they noticed the stark difference between themselves and their American counterparts on this front indicates the ubiquity of the issue for Americans.

The presence of this struggle within the identity of the American veteran and the reasons behind it are the topic of this chapter. We will explore the phenomenon as it was presented to us by the interviewees and draw connections that might help us understand its sources. There are three things that we will consider in this chapter—identity constriction (the experience of being reduced to a military member either within one's own mind or by society), identity expansion (the experience of being able to integrate one's military identity with one's civilian identity and being able to see military service as expanding rather than constricting), and identity coercion (the experience of being coerced into loyalty to one's military identity). Our goal here is to show how these things appear within American military culture and how this is often juxtaposed in the experience of our NATO allies.

## IDENTITY CONSTRICTION

One of the things that were prevalent in our interviews was the presence of what we will term identity constriction. Identity constriction (similar to affect constriction) is when one's identity is reduced to a singular facet in a way that becomes rigid and limiting. For example, when one identifies as a Marine in such a constrictive way that they can *only* see themselves as a Marine and other parts of their identity fall away partially or entirely. In this section, we will examine examples of identity constriction and discuss the ways in which it can get in the way of the reintegration process. This constriction can be seen in tiny areas of life that may not seem especially important—but the restriction that it represents is quite significant. When one's identity is constricted to a facet that they can no longer participate in, the effects can be devastating.

For example, an American servicemember details this in his fellow veterans in the following way:

> [Other veterans are] all running around with camo. It makes it feel like, makes me feel like I'm back in the military and I have to tell a private not to wear his dog tags to the strip club or something like that. Don't wear your tan shirt to the strip, you know what I mean? I'm not judging them for it, but it's like, c'mon dude. You got to represent something else.

While wearing camo or tags when it is no longer necessary may seem like a benign behavior, this constant signaling of military status to oneself and those around him can make it difficult to transition out of military identity. Further, this inability to feel at home as a civilian can make one's identity feel impossible altogether. This can make the veteran feel disoriented, socially isolated, and can lead to suicidality:

> Regarding suicide, I have thought that it's almost like they didn't recognize their own self in the mirror. After their service, when they got home, the outside just didn't fit the inside. On the inside, they were soldiers, but on the outside, they were just Joe Shmoe. And maybe a lot of that had to do with how they identified and actualized themselves. Maybe foreign soldiers, they're more of a citizen, so they don't see themselves as a soldier first. They're family-oriented first or

> whatever it is that they're doing. I don't know a ton about foreign militaries, but I don't think there is the same ideal of soldier first, or Marine first. Once a Marine always a Marine type of thing. It didn't seem to be that way when we were down range with those guys. From everything that I've observed, these [American] guys come home, and they don't see themselves or recognize themselves. The image they project to society is not what they feel on the inside. I think they struggle with that more than anything. It's not necessarily the combat or the dead bodies, explosions or the wounds—it's identity shift. It's like a paradox of their own identity.

Again, though these may seem like minor benign behaviors, what they represent is paramount. When one's identity becomes a paradox—an unsolvable contradiction—this can make life feel impossible in general. In the previous chapter, we described how some of our NATO ally countries build more of a dual identity in their military personnel. When one starts out as a citizen-soldier in training, perhaps it is easier to return to that status again after serving.

It is also striking that this American veteran does not believe it is combat-related trauma causing these high suicide rates for veterans. Instead, it is the deepening identity crisis that is causing this sense of disorientation for American veterans. He describes how American veterans might feel a deep sense of pride in their military identity; however, they are not able to actualize this form of identity in any meaningful way once they return to civilian life. This is at least in part because while military *status* brings social capital in America, military *life* is neither understood nor embraced in American civilian culture.

In other words, a tension lies at the very heart of being an American veteran. While *to be a veteran* means something, *what it means to be a veteran* is utterly misunderstood. While there is social capital promised by carrying the status of veteran, there is no real value behind this capital. Accordingly, the veteran is left in tension as well—the only choices are to either cling to this identity or accept that it was meaningless all along. It seems logical to cling to this identity when given the alternative, but one's tendency to exclusively hold on to veteran identity while no longer actively serving causes further disorientation and isolation. Statements like the one mentioned above, "Once a Marine, always a Marine," are thought to be a deeply helpful mindset in the training and mobilization process; however, it becomes a haunting limitation when one comes home.

Identity constriction is amplified by the stereotypes that exist with American culture. These stereotypes—which have been crafted by singular and outdated conceptions of veterans and then are reified by the intensity of the military/civilian divide—are harmful not just because they are inaccurate but because they are reductionist caricatures. An American describes one such stereotype—that of the "disgruntled veteran":

> I make fun of my friends all the time for it. That pride around being a disgruntled veteran, ya know? I'm maladjusted, leave me alone. That kind of stuff is toxic. I see it a lot. Younger guys I worked with who committed suicide. That's a staple mindset. I notice it the most among younger guys, especially if the military is the only thing they have done and identified with. I get guys calling me up in the night, telling me stuff all the time. They're struggling, but they won't talk to their friends or family about it. I think there's an element of protecting the symptom. Even with the combat aspect of things, they protect it.

This veteran describes a toxic form of identity constriction among veteran communities. This constriction makes reintegration impossible on several levels—most striking is the protection of the symptom. The constriction makes it impossible for the veteran to fully disclose his or her experiences, struggles, and narrative accounts to civilians. "Protecting the symptom," then, is simply another way of insulating oneself from having to be seen and known by others.

While identity constriction can happen after deployment and get in the way of reintegration, it can also happen to soldiers while they are still on active duty. Many veterans come into service with military career goals that go unmet because of job availability, injury, or other obstacles. An American veteran describes his struggle with adapting to limited positions after an injury:

> I just felt everything starting to go. They offered me an administration job. . . . I'm gonna be looked at as broken in the unit and you can't get away from that stuff. I'm not a pencil pusher. In the military, [if I did an administrative job] I would feel like a total douchebag. I just don't want to be that guy.

This veteran went on to have success as an operations sergeant but still held a negative conception of himself and felt frustration at his injury and its repercussions. His language here is stark and reveals deep shame and fear of judgment from others. While it is certainly normal to feel frustration when injury prevents one from doing what one intended, this lasting shame seems to represent an inability to see one's own identity beyond this singular goal.

To be sure, identity constriction is reified by societal stereotyping. While it is true that veterans constrict their own identities in part, it is also true the American understanding of the veteran is quite restrictive. When veterans are constantly othered by stereotypes in civilian society, it becomes even more difficult to identify as a citizen, or a citizen-soldier. An American veteran shared his experience being reduced and stereotyped:

> In certain classes, people would be like, "Let's just call on [the veteran] for that perspective." Which is fine. But when it becomes a thing like a novelty. It's just that there's way more to me than that. I don't feel like it's a good representation of me. So, then it was just something I tried to avoid. I don't want to be viewed as the veteran guy. There was one time I couldn't get an appointment with the guidance advisors office, the lady at the desk literally wrote, "Angry veteran came in wanted to speak with Corina, was upset with her hours." I wasn't angry and I didn't want to be seen as a veteran. I was a student who had questions.

Since our identities are not simply developed in a vacuum but arise in and around our experiences with others, the way that other people see us and the stories they tell about us become a part of who we are. If the veteran is struggling to reintegrate his military identity with his civilian identity, and then is consistently reminded that he is only a veteran—and that there is only one way to be a veteran—this can complicate the process as well as contribute to feelings of isolation and shame.

There is another phenomenon which accompanies and amplifies identity constriction, which is that the skills that one learns in many military positions are not terribly transferrable after leaving the military. Since there is little infrastructure to help veterans link their military identity with their next position, this leaves them feeling that they need to justify themselves in their new identity. This was corroborated across cultures in our research. A British veteran explained:

> In the UK, I'd say, especially in if you do special forces work like I realized once I got outside that its really cool to see on paper, but civilian jobs aren't interested in if we can kick a house in or parachute out of a helicopter. Like our qualifications, they just don't really transfer over.

There is consensus across combat MOS veterans through each nation interviewed in this study. The skill sets formed in the combat arms are not easily transferrable to civilian careers and civilian engagements upon leaving active service. However, despite echoing these sentiments, NATO ally veterans were much more likely to have some anticipation of life after combat. This likely insulates them from aligning their whole identity with the military.

For American veterans, on the other hand, the lack of transferability of their skills combined with the other factors at play can elevate the identity shift after combat to the level of full identity crisis. As an American veteran describes:

> I did two deployments. I did one to Iraq and one to Afghanistan. For me the issue came when I switched out of active duty to go to college because I had a

> complete identity shift and that was much more difficult. Before when people asked me, "What do I do." I would be like, "Oh, I'm a soldier." It was a very strong structured identity. Now people ask and I say "Oh, I'm a college student," but I couldn't say that, especially the first semester where I haven't really proved that I could do college, that I could achieve grades, that I could perform and be successful. It was difficult because I wasn't sure of my own identity there. I would call it an identity crisis. I would say the first semester I struggled until I got my grades back and I did very well. I got like all A's and a B+. Something like that. I've gotten on dean's list every single semester, so to me that was like my proof that I could do it, and its where it's supposed to be.

While this veteran had the potential of another kind of identity waiting at the ready for him, not every servicemember has a ready-made life awaiting. It is also notable that the veteran did not feel comfortable calling himself a student until he had proven himself to be a capable one.

To summarize, what is at stake when it comes to identity constriction across cultures seems to be two questions: what does it mean to be a soldier, and what does it mean to have been a soldier? Both questions are posed to both the individual who has served and those who surround him. Without the ability to move fluidly around one's self-concept and see oneself (and accordingly be seen by others) as simultaneously a solider, veteran, and citizen, one's identity becomes fixed and restrictive.

## IDENTITY EXPANSION

If identity constriction lies at one end of the spectrum, identity expansion lies at the other extreme. Identity expansion can be said to happen when healthy reintegration occurs and the veteran is able to see their military service as a part of their larger identity—indeed, an identity that has been enhanced and expanded by service rather than constricted. A German veteran describes the two poles:

> There are the ones who, I don't know, more or less stayed [in the military]. So, whatever they do when I see pictures of them or hear what they do, it was so shaping of an experience for them that it's still accompanied them somehow. So, when I see pictures of them living or doing this outdoor adventure things, posting pictures of being in the woods, they are still wearing their military uniform. And, then I see others who were able to just see it as a small part on the scale of life. They came back from Afghanistan, it was over for them, and they just moved on. I don't know how I can say that, but it was just a job for them. I mean they were *all* really good soldiers. It's just. Some moved on and some stayed.

The first group described here is in line with identity constriction—this is the disoriented veteran who is experiencing an inability to see himself as anything other than soldier after deployment. Here we see someone's military identity is at war with his civilian identity, making the integration of these two identities impossible. This can be seen in the way that these individuals engage in civilian life, carrying their military status with them as a way to both anchor and explain themselves.

The second group described here are the veterans who are not experiencing identity constriction, and therefore are able to embrace their civilian lives after the military, and also to integrate the previous identity construct with it. Rather than needing to carry the anchor of military status into civilian life, they can see it as a part of their larger identity and therefore no longer need to signal to it. It is important to note that the German veteran saw no distinction between these groups while deployed. In other words, it is not the case that those who are less actively engaged when deployed have an easier time reintegrating. Rather, it seems that those who were able to see their experience as identity expanding rather than constricting were able to move fluidly in between roles.

A key part of what distinguishes those who struggle with identity constriction rather than identity expansion seems to be whether or not they have a variety of previous life experiences. Those who had other jobs and careers tended to have an easier time toggling back and forth between sometimes competing identities. An American veteran who joined the army relatively late in life, deployed, and then returned back to civilian life describes how his previous experience helped him adapt:

> I was 32 when I originally joined the army, so I had already had an adult life behind me—my value was not in any way predicated on my experience in the military and I left it behind very quickly. I don't love what I do now but I already scratched the adrenaline itch earlier in life. I joined later in life. I didn't get conditioned into the shit the way 18-year-olds do. I always knew that I would do something else after (the military) was over. For now, this is fine. I'm o.k. with that.

For this veteran, his life experience and age likely offered him a unique sense of perspective that those who join before life experience do not have. Previous careers and life experience made it so that when he joined the military, military service hadn't been the only facet of his life that was meaningful. As the German above described, to this veteran, serving in the military was just another job—not the epitome of his identity. One that he loved and took pride in doing well, but not much different than what he had done before or what he would do after.

While it is helpful to see that having a rich life and previous experience can aid in the reintegration process and potentially help avoid identity constriction, this is not a realistic goal for the military—there will always be those who enlist early and before having had much life experience outside of the military. For those who struggle with a univocal commitment to their military identity, what kinds of practices can be put in place to prevent this from becoming a major barrier to reintegration? A possible answer lies in the experience of our NATO ally veterans. For example, a Norwegian veteran described his experience with identity constriction, but also detailed how this constriction did not persist for him because of the extensive time off immediately following his contract:

> It was a little bit hard because after one year you are like, you are not the same, I think. Your mind is just changed; you come back like a military man. And when you come back everything changes. How can I say that? You feel like a stranger in the city. When you meet some friends, some old friends, they say that you are not the same. You've changed. Not in a really bad way just your mind has changed a bit. It's like you don't have a real personality. When I was in the army, you don't have a place for your personality. You have your job and you have to do it and that's all. So, when I came back, I was conditioned like that. I woke up every day at 6 in the army. Returning to civilian life was hard at first but I felt I was adjusted after a few months. I think that now I am normal. I had like three months of vacation time at the end of my contract. I went to Japan.

There are several points worth noting here. First, Norwegian veterans are able to take a "vacation" at the end of their active duty contracts. This period of time is one in which the servicemember is still technically on active duty and being paid but does not have day-to-day military obligations. This is available to Israeli and German servicemembers as well—many of whom reported that this time was critical in processing their deployment experiences and reintegrating back into civilian society.

Second, this Norwegian veteran describes feeling deeply changed from his military service time. He describes a breakdown and restructuring of his personality. The idea that one may be changed by their time in service cannot be avoided or entirely prevented. However, though these changes took place and this veteran did struggle for a few months, he ultimately was able to feel "normal" and comfortable. In other words, his identity constriction did not follow him for long. This was a theme throughout this research—while NATO allies described almost identical experiences as American veterans, the intensity and duration was much different.

An Israeli veteran commented on his time off after the military and how critical it was when he was ending his service and permanently integrating back into society:

> As soon as you finish the military service, so me and my group we organized a vacation to Thailand, let's say and then we continued but it's really a thing that people are doing here that after the service we get some money from the service. Not much but then you take a long vacation to South America, or to India, or to Australia, wherever you want. And that's something that I think is superb really because it gives you a break after an intense period of time. You see a bit of the world. Other cultures. You learn a lot and then you're more determined, more motivated to start working or whatever. The vacation is really important for us because when we serve it's our country and we love it and we have to protect it but we know it's like a pause, a break, in our life and that after that there are tons, tons of programs for rehabilitation and stuff. Programs to put you back into civilian life, to help you integrate back. . . . So, near the end of the three years you have people who are coming for jobs, like programs for studies and everything. Which expands a little bit of the civilian life in Israel abroad. . . . So, I had this whole surrounding that helped me integrate back into the civilian life.

This veteran served in the Israeli special forces, one of the most combat-heavy and combat-intense military units in existence. Despite multiple combat deployments in a short period of time, his reintegration to Israeli civilian life was described as quite smooth and even seamless. Among several factors he credits the Israeli military "vacation" as a major factor in this process.

Israeli servicemembers are offered several months at the end of their active duty contract to take an extended respite from their active duty obligations. They are also paid during this time and are given little restrictions on where they can go with their leave. This veteran, like many others, enlisted at eighteen years of age, and so did not have the benefit of much previous life experience to help him contextualize his military identity. However, the vacation offered him an additional expansion of identity that gives room for processing and growth. Many report that these vacations give them experiences of diversity, culture, civilian life, and new perspectives on foreigners. The sense of expansion offered here undoubtedly supports the process in moving away from identity constriction and into identity expansion, making the reintegration process much easier.

## IDENTITY COERCION

One of the things that stood out as uniquely American was a coercion from within the military to cling to one's military identity by actively staying in the military. If the servicemember made the decision to leave, they were often admonished and shamed for this. As we have seen, making the shift from military back to civilian is already sufficiently complicated for American servicemembers, without this extra layer of coercion. The message behind this behavior is twofold—first, it is meant to convey that there simply is nothing meaningful beyond a military career, so to leave it is to make a serious mistake. Second, it further reifies the idea that to be an active military member is fundamentally different than it is to be a civilian. Making someone choose between one identity and the other strengthens the fear that they are not compatible and cannot be integrated.

It is important to emphasize not only that this coercion is not limited to peer interactions but that this messaging often comes through senior leadership. An American describes this in the following way:

> So, they were doing everything to keep me in, including negative things. They were like, you are gonna fail, you're gonna come back because you will fail out of college. You're going to go work at McDonalds. [This was] the retention people. The people who come around and talk to you about retention when you got like less than a year of time left. And they do carrot and stick but they always way more stick than carrot. So like some of it is like that "where there's guy who's staying in the military for 20 years?" and I told him I don't want to be in the military, he may feel like I'm telling him the military is crap, and its offensive to him. So, their response might not be like great. They might be like, okay that's fine that's your preference or they might be like, "this guy says the military sucks and I've chosen this as my profession, well screw him, I am going to tell him he is going to fail." There are always psychological pieces to this. But I heard that my entire career when I was active, whenever I would talk about getting out.

Undoubtedly, it is disturbing to look into the American military's culture of dismissal toward civilian life and veterans' abilities to succeed in civilian culture. Given what we already know about the intense familial connections within the military, it is clear why these sentiments might echo in the conscience of young men and women as they leave the active service. Americans reported that when they hit roadblocks in civilian life—bad days at work, frustrations with a boss or coworker—they wondered if their peers and superiors had been right and they had made the wrong decision after all.

The only other NATO ally country that described any amount of pressure was a Canadian servicemember who describes this in the following way:

> There was a bit. They were kind of grooming me to be a manager and then one of the senior noncommissioned officers and I remember a few instances where they "Lost my paperwork." They were basically begging you to find another contract because they said they would give me relocation preference, training preference, and all these preferences to basically get me to stay. I did my time,

> so I said I'm gonna be moving on. Inevitably, they just let me go without much pressure.

Though this experience was slightly pressuring, notice that there is nothing like the negativity and speculation that are present in the American accounts. In other NATO ally countries, this pressure was so absent that the idea of it was difficult for them to understand at first. Consider the following account from an Israeli veteran:

> My family was really glad that I left after three years. But from the officers and everything I didn't feel any pressure. They said it's something you can be good at if you want to, you have this and this, but it's up to you. And that's it basically so no pressure.

Again, though this veteran does express some sense of pressure as he transitioned, his narrative is not nearly as severe as that offered by his American counterparts above. Ultimately, his retention officers use bureaucratic measures to hold up his transition, as opposed to psychological shame. Finally, in a culture with mandatory service, there simply isn't as much pressure put on the military structure of Israel to keep servicemembers in when their contracts are up.

## CONCLUSION

When soldiers come home from war, they face a new kind of battle. This is the battle of integrating their military and civilian identities. The word "reintegrate" comes from the Latin *reintegrare*, which means to renew, to reinstate. They must restore their lives to unity again. Though we think of homecoming as a joyful occasion, reintegration is no small task. Though this has likely been an issue for as long as there have been wars to come home from, recent studies have given empirical justification to the theoretical idea that finding identity unity after war is a struggle. Though many servicemembers come home and do not struggle, studies suggest that between 40 percent and 62 percent of returning veterans struggle with reintegration to some degree, and that 25 percent of them struggle intensely (Sayer et al., 2010, 2014, 2015).

There have been attempts to figure out why reintegrating into civilian life post-war is so difficult, and each point to a different source of difficulty. Some point to the taxing realities of war on both the servicemember and the family (Hutchinson & Banks-Williams, 2006; Bowling & Sherman, 2008). Others blame our contradictory social mores that demand that servicemembers remain simultaneously heroically pure while they commit what we normally deem atrocities (Shay, 1994, 2003, 2014).

While these are surely a part of the problem, we were looking for potentially hidden sources of struggle when it comes to identity reintegration. In this chapter, we articulated three facets of reintegration that we have not seen in the literature. The first was identity constriction—the experience of being reduced to a military member only at the cost of the other facets of one's identity. In our NATO ally countries, as well as in successful reintegration stories from American veterans, we found the opposite of identity constriction, which we termed identity expansion. The third facet which further complicates identity constriction, making expansion nearly impossible, was identity coercion—being coerced into a singular identity source.

## *Chapter 3*

# Solidarity

Many veterans face a serious void in their life upon leaving active duty or deployment. Specifically, they often struggle with the difficulty of replicating the types of relationships they forged with members of their platoon when moving into a civilian career (Ahern, Worthen, Masters, Lippman, Ozer, & Moos, 2015; Junger, 2010; Kukla, Rattray, & Saylers, 2015; Browning, 2015; Nelson Goff, Crow, Reisbig, & Hamilton, 2007; Friedman, 2005; Demers, 2011; Caddick, Phoenix, & Smith, 2015; Monson, Taft, & Fredman, 2009; Bowling & Sherman, 2008). Though these struggles are often not directly connected to traditional conceptualizations of PTSD, symptoms and struggles may arise for servicemembers that are consistent with the range of symptoms often tied to PTSD.

PTSD is the most common diagnosis for servicemembers who experience symptoms and struggles upon reintegrating into civilian life. However, what is often less accounted for in the conceptualization of these symptoms is the possibility that a veteran is experiencing symptoms related to PTSD but *not as a result of standing witness to a traumatic event.* Beyond the experience of standing witness to unexpected trauma in war, there are other social and motivational struggles the reintegrating servicemember may face when returning from active duty.

The moment of reintegration is perhaps the most complicated in the career span of a servicemember. It is here where the effects of training, deployment, and military identity overlap with any cultural and societal issues that may be present. When these effects and issues become layered, they can create significant barriers to reintegration—barriers that are especially difficult to tease out and treat when their etiology is not well understood. Here we will attempt to illustrate how difficult these barriers are, and how the barriers facing American servicemembers are especially difficult to overcome.

In order to study this across cultures, we have focused on the concept of solidarity at three points—in training, while on deployment, and upon returning home. We looked at both the solidarity (or lack thereof) that one felt with peers and the solidarity (or lack thereof) that one felt with civilians. We coded solidarity in this study as any reference to the general level of commonality, trust, connectedness, unity, and support one felt. Strikingly, there were little to no significant differences in these descriptions across countries, cultures, or branches of service.

To summarize our findings, which will be spelled out in further detail below, there are three major trends that we found. The first was that without exception, all participants in this study felt a palpable level of solidarity within their military units. Furthermore, though certainly not all, the overwhelming majority of participants in this study described feeling difficulty in replicating the sense of solidarity experienced in one's military career to the relationships one experienced in civilian life after military service.

The second trend that we saw was that American veterans uniformly felt that an inability to feel solidarity with civilians was the fault of civilians. Often this gap was attributed to civilians lacking the ability to comprehend military service and military culture. Generally speaking, there was little hope that this could be changed. However, though NATO ally veterans also experienced a lack of solidarity with civilians in comparison to their military relationships, NATO ally veterans were far more likely to either take responsibility for that distance and/or trust that this distance was a temporary state of events that would decrease over time. Overall, as they gained more time in civilian culture, NATO allies felt far less distance from civilians in their country than American veterans did. Americans who were able to form solidarity with civilians were either willing to take accountability for the lack of unity and commonality or were optimistic about their ability to form stronger relationships over time.

The third trend that we found was that the veterans who were able to form stronger bonds of solidarity with civilians were typically those who had a far less univocal commitment to their identity as a veteran after leaving the military. As we discussed in detail in the previous chapter, for the most part, almost all NATO ally participants were able to ameliorate any univocal commitment to veteran identity after leaving active duty service. On the other hand. American veterans struggled much more with no longer seeing themselves as identified with the military after leaving. We suggest that one's commitment to identity likely had a significant effect on one's ability to form strong relationships of solidarity and to be open to civilian perspectives and culture after leaving the military.

## SOLIDARITY WITH THE PLATOON

As previously mentioned, strong social support and a sense of relational connection have been critically examined by both our previous work and the greater field of researchers studying veterans and military psychology. Therefore, we hypothesized that veterans solicited for this project would likely describe a strong sense of unit solidarity derived from their military and, especially, deployment experiences. We were unsure of just how the nuances of this closeness might be articulated from one nation to the next; however, there was very little difference in describing this sense across all forty participants from all six nations. Here is a representative sample:

American 1:

> [My platoon] were my family. I'm sure you hear that every time you ask this question. They were people I would do anything for. And they would go out of their way to fucking help me. I miss the camaraderie. I don't miss the military; I don't miss not having a mission to prepare for because then it's just a lot of big army stuff. Sit through this briefing, sit through this video, we have to check the box on this, or we have this to do. But, when you're training for a deployment and you have a mission and something to do its exciting, and I miss that life. But I think what I miss the most is the camaraderie, it's the guys who you're doing it for.

American 2:

> I felt I was always very close to my unit. It felt more like a family than friends I felt like. A lot of time I felt like I had more friends in my unit than not. We all felt very close. But sometimes there's those people you love to hate too. Like there was this one guy that I came . . . we basically did our first immunization together, we did everything together, we deployed together, we ironed our shirts together and it was like my brother. But I like hated him at the same time. Yet, I wouldn't go to anyone else for help or anything. But I would definitely tell people at the time that I didn't like him as a person.

German 1:

> I don't think that [that level of camaraderie] will ever happen again, I guess. Which is sad in a way but this is what all the others say too, yeah? Even if I meet them some years later, they are like okay this was unique in a way, yeah? And I think this really only happens if you are really in an extreme situation like in a combat mission. So, it has not only advantages. The closeness of my company was really strong in Afghanistan. So, we were so proud and so close together that our old guys around us were just

stupid and I don't know, lazy and we were the only ones, you know? This was the feeling, yeah? So, the closer you are together, the more you disconnect from your surrounding in a way. The others were the stupid ones and we were the good ones. And even what I said, when we came back to Germany this comradeship from more or less one day to the other ended because we came back and then there were ones who left the army and the next ones were deployed to other areas, I don't know, other parts of Germany. And it ended very, very fast after the mission. All in all, I don't think that I will ever experience something like that again. Except when there will be war or whatever. Which is a bit sad okay, there certainly is a disconnection feeling to German society.

British 1:

You've been somewhere and done something that you could never compare it to with anyone else. Like your civilian friends they only know their day or whatever. When I was with my [platoon] mates it was like, I felt on top of the world.

Norway 1:

It's really in the training. Waking up early, going through exercise every morning, and training hard throughout the day. It forms a strong sense of identity and brings you close to the people you are going through it with. I felt very close to the people I served with at that level and still do.

Canadian 1:

I was super close with them but especially with the guys in your section. You have a section of roughly twelve guys and you are more close with those guys than the rest of the platoon based on work relationship, you're doing things with your section a lot more. On the whole everyone was family.

Canadian 2:

It's not comparable. When you're in infantry rifle sections, like you're legitimately family. All be it, a super dysfunctional family with a crazy, authoritarian father—but like your little dysfunctional, retarded family with your retarded brothers and your super smart brother and your nerdy brother and, or sister like in Canada, but it's like the connection you have with those people like sharing a blanket in the freezing rain, like undergoing extreme training, like sharing a blanket in the freezing rain—sharing a little ranger blanket that you guys call a woobie—like sharing a sleeping bag at like -30 because you almost got burned up and you know like who the hell help? Like you've got a tic on your face and you can't reach it.

> You know, you gotta be like "Hey buddy, I need a solid. I got this tic on my face. Could you get it?" And they're like "Sure, no problem." You know, like would you walk up to the doctor's office or another researcher and be like, "Hey buddy, so, I've got a tic on my face. Could you get it for me?" So, it's not comparable. It totally isn't. In the infantry, you have no choice but to get close cause your life fully depends on the other person. It's like being a police officer. Your life fully, totally depends on the guy next to you, on your partner or —. I miss that. I do miss the connection. I do. I know a lot of guys who suffer from it even more. I don't suffer from it. I do miss it but I'm kinda like "Yeah, it's not the same." You end up gravitating toward other veterans because you just have that connection and it just feels good now and again. It just feels good to be in the arms of another human being and you know, I think all people—civilians and military alike—we, as human, crave and need connection with other humans. Like we need it, otherwise you're a little bit of a sociopath, no?

Six consistent themes that were present across these passages. First, participants felt a deep and even familial sense of connection to former platoon members. Second, participants often said that though they did not miss military life, on the whole, they almost always reported that they missed the people they served and deployed with. Connected to this, the third theme was that even when platoon unity and solidarity were not ideal, participants still valued the relationships of former platoon members far more than their civilian relationships. Fourth, participants expressed a sense that they could communicate clearly with a shared sense of language and purpose with veterans and, especially, former platoon members. Fifth, many participants expressed that it was either the hard training of military life or the deployment experiences that served as the primary catalysts for building solidarity within a unit.

Finally, there was a general sense of fatalism around any ability to recreate a similar sense of solidarity with civilians. Almost all veterans said that they would never have that kind of connection again. Though there were relative degrees of difference across cultures, the majority of participants across the spectrum expressed how there was a sense that it would be difficult if not impossible to replicate the sense of solidarity experienced with former servicemembers.

We deliberately chose to offer passages from across the spectrum of NATO ally participants to emphasize the ubiquitous nature of these sentiments. Each passage speaks similarly to the intimacy experienced by many servicemembers within a unit through training and deployment settings. This is especially relevant because what it suggests is that it is not the irreplaceability of this camaraderie alone that causes American veterans to struggle so deeply with reintegration. While veterans from all countries experienced similar levels of intimacy and unparalleled connection and camaraderie, only American veterans had lasting difficulties finding a connection with civilians.

## LACK OF SOLIDARITY WITH CIVILIANS

As we hypothesized in the outset of this project, the strength and solidarity of veterans' relationships to the members of their former units would likely be juxtaposed by disconnection and a lack of solidarity with civilians upon reintegration. What we were unsure about was how this would be reported in NATO ally veterans. As we saw when we looked at identity in the previous chapter, NATO ally veterans might have struggled a bit with these things, but American veterans had lasting difficulties that had significant impacts on their quality of life. Overall, American veterans experienced a greater and more lasting sense of detachment and a near-complete lack of solidarity with civilians. Again, while some NATO ally veterans had similar struggles, they understood them differently and also did not experience them for as long a period of time.

Below is a representative sample:

American 1:

> Things were very stiff at first. More so with my stepmother, my brother and sister and I. You get so used to being as brief as possible. She would say that I was being hateful. But I wasn't, I didn't mean anything by it. So, I kind of had to change that up and not be so short with people. It's not a personal thing. So, I definitely think I've come out of and gone full circle with that. I'm not a bubbly chatty Cathy but like . . . I think that I've come to terms with the fact that I'm a quiet person now. Not that I was very bubbly and outgoing before but things just weren't as real. I think that everyone kind of realizes the separation that I'm trying to make. There was who I was before and there's who I am now.

American 2:

> You know, I do try to be in a team with [civilians]. I think that one of the reasons why veterans have such a hard time going to college when they get back from the military is you're not a part of a team at all anymore. Like, you're truly on your own. And I feel like some of the people that are most accepted in the military are team-oriented people. And the people who are the least accepted in the military are the ones who are more individualistic, you know?

American 3:

> The best way I can describe it is when I returned from a deployment it was good having the national guard still there because you had people you connected with. My civilian friends and family who hadn't been in the military, I was looking at them through a fog. I didn't feel connected to civilians at all. It's kind of look at it through a window or fog. It's like the feeling of a woman going through childbirth, you can't really identify with it, she can describe it was best as she can and you can try to sympathize but unless you go through it, you don't get it. . . . So, when I came home, I would go to school. I treated that like a business transaction, I didn't socialize with anybody. And then my work I didn't work with a lot of people. When I was removing junk, the lady who owned the company, I deployed with her kid. So, he'd show up and work sometimes. I suppose I had it better than a lot of people when they come home. But again, the guys that I work with that haven't deployed have their strong suits and they bring things to the table that I don't. . . . the only time I feel the real disconnect is when they do the run around of "oh I almost joined the military but, . . ." or they ask me if I know someone who they know in the Army.

American 4:

> Yeah, so there was definitely a disconnect when I got to college. I was very fortunate. I took advantage of school right after my last deployment. So, there was a group of veterans that were all kind of in the same boat. Unconsciously we all started to gravitate towards each other. When we started talking, we realized that, you know, that all of our service periods were kind of close together. You know, the past couple years. Everybody had done the same thing, so it was a support group that I didn't know I was going to have. You know, I think things probably would have been different if I didn't have that support group or didn't go to school. If I hadn't tried to jump back into a routine, it would have been different.
>
> I feel there's a difference between, you know, vets that are coming back and becoming students and then just kids graduating from high school and then jumping into college. Personally, I try not to make that separation. I feel like it doesn't help my reintegration back into society, so I really try to keep an open mind. Like hey listen, that was their choice and this was my choice to join. I think everyone's got their own path. However, I definitely feel like when we get into political debates, especially in my undergraduate career, we'd get a lot of political debates. I did feel resentful when other student would say something that was kind of out of their way or they really didn't have the full picture. They'd say something that was misinformed because they weren't there. I really tried not to be too

confrontational. But after somebody would say something that I thought was, you know, really inaccurate or really inappropriate, then I'd kind of mark that person and be like alright well you have no idea. So, I won't write you off but, I'm not even going to try to explain myself.

I am still nervous to work with people who were not in the military. I feel like, you know, I'm always questioning my soft skills, I'm always questioning if I'm pushing people too far, you know? Am I acting too military, is my mindset still in military mode? And I'm constantly cognizant of you know, just keep it dialed down, you know, you can't act a certain way. If there's conflict, you can't really react the same way. It won't really settle in the same way that it will in the military. There's HR processes. It just, it's a completely different mindset. So yeah, I'm definitely still working on that. But it makes the transition a lot easier when your employer is prior military as well. At least you guys are kind of going through that journey together.

American 5:

Coming back, it was difficult, my problem wasn't so much getting reacclimated and getting back to work, working was easy for me because I was focused—it was speaking to other people. Military people, and specifically infantry people have their own language, things that other people would find rude or repulsive was seen as a common joke. And we made it through that way, it was a way of "embracing the suck." The other thing I found was that there were no secrets. If there was a problem, your buddies would bring it up and you'd talk about it, and then there wouldn't be a problem anymore, because everyone there was moving through it with you and it was a total community. Other than working with other veterans or like-minded people, like at the gym for example, even at work I don't feel anywhere near the same type of camaraderie that I've felt in active duty, the reserves, or with my veteran friends. [With civilians] I can't speak freely . . . in my mind, I have to always be careful of what I say because it might insult somebody or make them uncomfortable. Something I might think is funny, or a situation that may have happened in the military, I have to kind of keep it low and PC because I'm afraid of insulting someone. I'm in an office atmosphere now, I have people behind me and next to me, always interacting and it's a good team as in focusing on the situation, it's not a good team as in I wouldn't go out and socialize with these people, or have a drink with them because you got your work life, your private life, your military life, and I don't want to merge these things together. I have acquaintances at work, and I'm fine with us not being friends. I don't mind being alone, I get things done and I'm focused more when I'm alone. Except with the military, I like to teach people and share information. It's the one place that I can relax a little bit.

British 1:

It was definitely very hard to interact when I got back because you're away for seven months in a completely different world. No one knows what goes on, especially in the U.K. It's just like you had just done this insane thing, and you get back, and then you just stood with normal people that couldn't give a dung care that you were away. They don't appreciate or respect that.

German 2:

When we arrived home, people started to live their own life and this was part of it. But also, the feeling of disconnection was much higher than it was when I returned home from Kosovo. It always a military mission the whole time. But with Afghanistan, it was feeling this little bit that people don't know what we are doing. There were confusing ideas of what our military was doing in Afghanistan. But there was no pressure to change that. Before Afghanistan I thought okay it's strange what people think of us—they don't really care—but I don't know that it's not a big thing. But as soon as our soldiers started to die in Afghanistan, citizens have to know because politicians who are voted by our society they sent us to these missions. And the people who vote for politicians should know what they sent us for more or less. They should know what they are doing to us more or less but they did not know.

Norway 1:

Even today, years later, I still feel just a bit different from civilians opted out of their mandatory service. I feel it because when I made some friends from the military it's different. A really close friend of mine who was also in the army with me, he's like in my close group of friends, and when we talk there's always a moment when we talk about the army and then it goes to 30 minutes or one hour. And all of the others are like, dude I don't understand what you're talking about. This is so boring, why do you have to talk about the army? I think sometimes you have some experience in the army so that really stays in your mind. And you have to talk about it when you're with your friends and I don't know why.

There are six trends in these passages to point out. First, all participants expressed a sense of distance from family members and loved ones, even suggesting that there was a significant change in these relationships when returning from active duty. Looking closely at the language though, American veterans experience this disconnection as lasting rather than temporary. Second, while there was some disconnection with civilians in all accounts, American veterans seemed to believe that civilians were more self-centered and less adept at teamwork on the whole. In other words, there is a sentiment that civilians are simply not capable of the kind of camaraderie experienced within the military.

Third, there is the idea that civilians were detached from the military experience in both American accounts and those of NATO ally countries—but in American veterans there seemed to be an experience of the lack of empathy toward both the mission and lived experience of war. NATO ally veterans might have pointed out a lack of political awareness, but this didn't seem to carry. Fourth, in America, there was little desire to have any intrinsic sense of connection to civilians and a sense that, at best, civilian relationships were seen as a means to an end. Fifth, there was a general sense among American veterans that civilians' opinions were naïve, misinformed, and/or ignorant. This led many participants, especially those who went to college after service, to readily dismiss the opinions of civilian peers in a classroom setting. Sixth, there was a relatively pervasive sense that veterans could not communicate freely with civilian peers. This was not unique to American veterans and it manifested in the areas of humor and political correctness, especially in the workplace. Moreover, participants expressed that there was a common lingo among veterans, one that was almost impossible to replicate with or communicate to civilians.

## THE UNIQUE AMERICAN EXPERIENCE: HATRED AS A BARRIER FOR REINTEGRATION

While it is clear that almost all veterans experience some kind of struggle reintegrating, American veterans struggled more intensely and for longer periods of time. Their struggle was more intractable—or at least it feels that way to them. Perhaps nothing was more representative of this than the hatred that American veterans reported feeling toward civilians. While NATO ally veterans might have expressed disappointment or frustration, it never raised to the level that it did consistently with Americans. Similar to the struggle with identity, this was something that American veterans self-reported, but it was striking enough to be noticed by other veterans as well. In many cases, the best case for American veterans was if they were able to *tolerate* civilians. American 1 describes this experience:

> I feel disdain for civilians, unfortunately. It is infuriating at times. I'm not big on crowds. I don't put myself around the masses. I can try to talk to people about it the best I can, but generally, those conversations don't go well.

This veteran seems resigned to the fact that he will never be able to relate to civilians without disdain. He refers to civilians as "the masses" which suggests a hierarchical relationship, and though he does not elaborate, when he does interact with "the masses" these conversations do not seem to yield any resembling connections.

American 2 presses the discussion forward, offering more nuance to these previously expressed sentiments:

> I had a lot of problems with people when I first got back to America. The things they complained about—it was like really? You have it so good here. Just stepping off the plane and seeing how green this country is and how much oxygen there is in the air. Compared to where I was—we basically have those floating bubble things that you see in sci fi. So, the ability to find things wrong with completely beautiful lives completely flabbergasted me. To be honest [civilians] are all soft bitches—and that's probably always going to be the case—but I don't have a problem with that and I've got nothing to prove. I've got my man card . . . nobody is going to take it from me. So, I can get along with people.

What is most striking about this passage is not the frustration toward naive civilians who have lost perspective on what true suffering is. Instead, it is the egregious generalization he proffers at the end of the passage—"they're all soft bitches." This view of civilians has to be an isolating mindset. We generally don't feel connected to those who we feel are less, or who are weak. Our relationships with them are built of necessity or pity rather than depth and compassion. It's also worth noting the tension in these statements. This veteran points out the incredible level of frustration that he encounters in these relationships—but then states that he doesn't have a problem with it. There's also the curious statement about the "man card" which he says he is not worried about, but if that is the case, why draw the distinction between the strong and weak in the first place?

American 3 presses these sentiments even further, ultimately articulating just how severe the chasm between his military relationships and his civilian relationships has become:

> You just muscle through it with your brain. You're just trying to stay on track in your brain. It's almost like you have to play out the conversation 3 times in your head before you actually say the words. . . . It gets frustrating when you let go and you let down your guard and you feel like you can let them in, and you let them behind the curtain and they find out that it's a little bit dark. Over time I've mastered being able to control the disconnect I felt. Now that I have a kid, I have to accept more things that you never thought of before. As you get older you find

> that some things are not as important to focus on . . . *even the person I disliked the most in my platoon I like better than the best friends I have at work now.*

There is a kind of exhaustion to this account. This veteran clearly feels that he cannot let down his guard at all around civilians, and that when he has done this it has not worked out well. Similar to the accounts above, this veteran seems totally resigned to this relationship with civilians and has no hope that it could be otherwise. Perhaps most striking in his account is his final sentence: "even the person I disliked the most in my platoon I like better than the best friends I have at work now."

American veterans also frequently pointed out their frustration with civilians when they did try and connect or ask them about their service. The fact that they did not connect in a real or authentic way was something that the veterans often found offensive and did not lead to connection. American 4 describes this sentiment:

> I hate when people are like "Oh, I almost joined the military but then I went to school" or "Oh, I had a brother who went in." It's like, "Dude, don't try to connect, that sucks." But, at the same time, I understood the military is not for everybody, it's just not. I would rather the people that didn't have the spine to do it, not do it. And it's not . . . there are just some people that fight and some people that don't.

This description contains quite a lot of disdain for civilians who did not join ("the people that didn't have the spine to do it"). It's also notable that civilians are simply not given the benefit of the doubt. Nowhere is the idea that perhaps civilians did not join the military because they were serving the country in some other essential way, or that their talents were better served elsewhere, or that they really were trying to connect by making reference to family members who served. There is a sense here that military service is the only form of serving one's country. Furthermore, unique to this passage is a sense of disdain for civilian attempts to try to connect or express empathy for joining. If you did not join, then don't waste time telling me about your family member's decision to join. There is an intense level of social isolation from civilians here, as well as a desire to only identify with individuals who have had the same exact life experience.

It would be logical to draw connections between the intensity of war and this simmering resentment that veterans feel when they come home and are largely surrounded by people who did not serve and do not understand. Surely this is a part of this phenomenon. However, it does not account for the level of disdain that American veterans feel toward civilians even during training.

Another American participant describes the way that he felt this sense of disdain for his civilian peers when he was an ROTC:

> Even when I was in ROTC, we had no right to be like that because we had really done nothing, we are just cadets. But we talk about civilians like we hate them and they piss us off. When we get up for PT at 5 am and we go to our eight am class after and there's some sorority girl complaining that the walk to class was cold and she was up to early, we are all like "fuck this person, we've been up since five and we were working out in this shit weather."

ROTC cadets are, arguably, at the lowest end of the food chain in the military hierarchy. They spend approximately four years trained, formed, and nurtured in a nondeployable training environment working toward their civilian and military educational goals. Undoubtedly, ROTC training environments can be austere and challenging; however, the nature of their training environment insulates cadets from the deeper commitments of mobilization that is in play for the rest of the military. Nevertheless, this American demonstrates how even in the initial training environment, a sense of disdain for and distance from civilian peers is present.

It is likely that the disdain comes from two sources in America—first, from within the military. There are clearly many points at which servicemembers are inundated with ideas about their superiority over civilians from training through deployment. Second, from disappointing interactions with civilians. The ignorance of civilians about the experience of combat leads to interactions that are inauthentic and stilted, and make the veteran feel misunderstood and undervalued. When these two sources are combined and reified throughout and after the servicemember's career, reintegration—even simple toleration—becomes nearly impossible.

## THE UNIQUE AMERICAN EXPERIENCE—FIGHTING TO FORM SOLIDARITY WITH CIVILIANS

As mentioned above, many participants—notably, the majority of American participants—expressed that they had become more or less resigned to this lack of solidarity with civilians. However, several NATO ally participants intentionally sought unique ways to overcome this social chasm. Though the majority of participants in this study expressed that they felt a lack of solidarity with civilians upon leaving active duty, NATO ally participants more often felt a sense of responsibility for this distance and actively worked to overcome it.

There is far less unanimity to the responses in this section as each participant had employed nuanced and subjectively valuable methods of engaging with civilians. However, what they all have in common is the sense of responsibility for confronting other civilians on this gap of connection and working to form a greater sense of unity, trust, and interconnectedness. Rather than resigning themselves to a life in which one is disconnected from all of those around him who did not go to war, they attempted to bridge the military/civilian gap.

This section will open with a lengthy passage from a German veteran describing the process he took to building his relationships with German civilians after deployment:

> This is actually what I try to tell the guys in the ministry of defense who think that I am the right one for them to do the marketing for the army. I tell them it's important to be honest and offensive. Just, let's face society with what we do and not hide and not be ashamed and not be too defensive. . . . I feel quite connected to civilians, but only because in my head a new topic or a new task grew, yeah? I'm involved [in a veteran's movement] and this was my first way for me out of that Afghanistan circle to get a better connection or better integration into German society. . . . So what I'm doing the whole day is to make people who live in the society somehow involved in the military, or make them interested in the military or something like that so I work on that, let's say line. So, I have a little fun there and I like it to be a little provocative and talk to people and to discuss with them about the military and our enemies. . . . So, I feel quite involved and I get the feeling that we create something connected at home.
>
> This new mission now was a chance to finish that Afghanistan mission. I mean it sounds maybe a little bit stupid to say that like six years later, but the mission wasn't over with coming back at least for me it was like still moving my mind all the time. And yeah, to now have a new mission makes it easier for me to end the other or it was easier, I ended it already. . . . This might be quite strange but the first thing where I really had the feeling of okay this was really nice now was when I gave my presentation at the university to the public. So, I did a presentation for everyone there. So, they filmed it and I invited my friends and my family too. And it was a big, big room in the university. And it was overcrowded so people were sitting on stairs, they were standing, and it was two and a half hours presentation that I give with discussion.

There are a couple of particularly notable things about this passage. The first is that in taking a position where this veteran is actively educating civilians about the military, he is able to find some space to bridge the gap between the military/civilian divide. Instead of judgment and disdain for civilians, his efforts have been directed at education and connection. Indeed, these efforts have helped him overcome any alienation that he might have felt when he first returned.

A Canadian veteran describes the adjustments that he had to make in order to reacclimate to civilian life below.

> Oh, you know, being a civilian now is nice. It's enjoyable. I more-or-less fit in. I can hide my army-ness pretty good. You know, I can let my hair grow a little long, get the hipster beard trim and you know, it's pretty wonderful actually, once you get over the fact that everybody's super lazy and only care about helping themselves. Yeah, basically, civilians are bad. But that feeling also comes from my current job which is not law enforcement but it's like security work and I work with law enforcement so it's like we get told to pretty much discover the earth all the time and you find there's some pretty terrible people out there but you know, I enjoy being out and if I was given the opportunity to get back in, I don't know if I would.
>
> I know that a lot of guys have a lot of difficulty reintegrating and fitting back in and they feel that civilians are lazy and basically, shitty people, and they don't do their part. They don't understand. They don't want to understand and it's like yeah that's true but that's also true in the Army. It's just in the Army, it's like bred out of you or beaten out of you whereas out here, it's you know, you're forced to deal with people because people can be themselves and you know, some people are selfish. Some people are generous, and some people have their blinders on, just ignore everything around them and only focus on what affects them so I mean it's a mixed bag but I like it.

This veteran unpacks some of the nuances of both civilian and military behavior and interaction. Though he is judgmental of civilians in some ways, there's more equanimity in his appraisal than we see in the accounts of the American veterans. As he says, selfishness and laziness are qualities that are espoused by military and civilian individuals in kind. It is striking that though he feels some similar sentiments to the American veterans described above, that settling on a much more nuanced account is much easier—and accordingly, makes his reintegration much easier.

Another Canadian describes his reintegration process similarly. He began by acknowledging that there is a unique bond formed in military service, especially as groups of individuals train together and experience trauma together. However, he went on to press back against the notion that these types of connections and experiences are wholly unique to military life and culture. Finally, in the passage below, he addresses what he believes as something like a desire for veterans to separate themselves and feel unique from civilians.

> I do feel connected now. It took a lot of time. It took a lot of work and it made a big difference. I think I could have stayed detached, but it took a lot of effort. I had to think, when you transitioning environments, it's like—one thing that really bothers me about veterans is this overblown sense of entitlement, you know, like "you don't know man, you weren't there." Or "I'm a veteran! I served!" You know, it's like "good for you buddy but you know, you're not in anymore. Nobody cares. It's time for you to shelf that and keep it in your drawer as an anecdote of a time in your life where you shined and now you gotta find something else to shine on." I went and I found something else that I'm passionate about and I love it and I just happen to find something that coincides that it turns out I'm doing something that is similar in nature to what I was doing before. You know, it's uh—yeah no I don't like the veteran culture we have now where everybody takes offense and everybody's like "You don't know what it's like." Like, what the heck, man? You don't have entitlement, man. You served. Good for you. That's fantastic but you know. A lot of people do their version of serving by working at (Canadian Company) every day and they're helping that corporation grow, you know and a preacher goes to church every day and he gives a talk and he helps people every day. At the end of every day lots of people are serving, not just veterans.

There is an almost kneejerk rejection of the notion that the veteran experience can never be empathized with or understood. This Canadian veteran expresses an unqualified affirmation toward the work of his civilian coworkers, as well as the greater population of all Canadian civilians who wake up with good faith and try to serve their community every day outside of military service. Not only is this mindset more nuanced and integrated, in general, but it undoubtedly helps when it comes to feeling connected to civilians after military service.

What we see in these three accounts, which are representative of most NATO ally veterans in this study, is that the alienating experience of the American veteran is not part and parcel of the experience of war. In fact, it is indeed possible to reintegrate with society and regain a feeling of connectedness post-combat. What seems to be necessary for this is a willingness to give up trappings of military culture that run counter to integration—trappings that are arguably more harmful than helpful in general. For example, working against any notion of being inherently superior to those who did not serve was helpful according to these accounts, as well as an openness to connecting with those who cannot have firsthand experience in combat.

## COPING AND FINDING SOLIDARITY—NATO ALLIES

As we have seen a lack of solidarity with civilians is a common theme for many veterans when they arrive home. What was relevant for our purposes are the ways that American veterans experienced this lack of solidarity when compared to our NATO ally veterans. What we found was that for Americans, this phenomenon of lack of solidarity is both more intense and also seems to last longer than for these other countries. Rather than a temporary phase that is a natural part of the reintegration process, it becomes a chronic problem that stands in the way of healing.

One of the things that stood out as especially unique were the appraisal patterns for the NATO ally veterans as compared to the American veterans. In this section, we will examine these different appraisal patterns with the goal of showing that though almost all participants in this study struggled to find solidarity with civilians after active duty service, European and Canadian NATO allies were far more likely to find coping mechanisms for this gap that made it less likely that they experience severe social isolation in their reintegration experience. It's not enough to simply note this—it is also helpful to notice specifically what these coping mechanisms were as we think about what we can change in American culture to alleviate some of this struggle.

A British veteran explains that though it was initially very frustrating to experience a gap between himself and civilians, that this frustration doesn't last—he was able to cope by accepting the natural differences between those who have served and those who have not:

> I think people notice I'll go out of my way and they wonder, like you are brought up that way? So, I'll go out of my way to help others, and then the time you need a favor you can guarantee they're gonna let you down. So, I just sort of accept that I guess. . . . There seems to be so much competition within civilian life like they are always trying to rat each other out or make someone look bad. You notice that and that sort of doesn't happen in the military and if you got a problem with someone in the military well, we are all human you're not gonna get along with everyone. You just gotta voice it out loud and try and solve it. [Some of the stuff] does piss me off, but . . . I have made peace with it. Even at my school, I'm one of the only ex-military guys, I don't really hang with the other guys and stuff. That's not me being antisocial like I'll talk to them and stuff from time to time but you know they're all like "let's all go out tonight" and I'm just like "Nah I'm gonna chill." I recognize it but it just doesn't bother me at the moment. Like I said, I'm busy studying.

There is an element of acceptance that we can see in this account—and was repeated in many other accounts of our NATO allies. Rather than looking for the same kind of camaraderie, connection, or support in civilian life, these veterans were able to recognize that it was not present, feel some of the disappointment in that realization, and then move on and accept it.

A Norwegian veteran expresses a similar sentiment and then arc of acceptance:

> I have some friends from the Army who are still my friends and they are like my brothers, I think. It's different from my friends from the unit or from school. There's a big difference. The difference is I didn't spend nine months training with my civilian friends. I didn't experience with my civilian friends what I did with my unit friends. I don't know how to say it but it's completely different. The training was really hard and that's what brings you together. Probably about six to nine months after I left the military, I no longer felt that sense of distance with civilians. [When I did feel] disconnected it was not because of someone who did something. When I came back what I remember is before I went to Germany, everyone used Facebook and when I came back it was like kind of old. Nobody used Facebook anymore. They had switched to Instagram or something like that. There were new apps and I felt isolated because I didn't understand what it was like. But after a month or two I was okay with it.

Similar to the American participants in this study, there was indeed an expressed sense of feeling palpably closer to military peers than civilians when returning to civilian life. However, unlike the American participants, the intensity and duration of this sense of distance are far less severe. In a relatively short period of time, Norwegian #1 is able to move past the initial feeling of disconnect to civilians and, at the time of the interview, expresses that he is more or less comfortable with his civilian life and relationships.

Again, he certainly acknowledges the gap in closeness, trust, and solidarity in his civilian relationships, but he is not deterred by this sense. He does not hold bitterness about it or think that things should be otherwise. What is especially interesting to note here is that there is a lack of judgment about the *character* of civilians. This Norwegian veteran is able to see that the closeness that he felt in connection with his platoon members was a result of the circumstances that formed their connection and is not a statement about who is a good person and who is not.

Another British veteran similarly acknowledges that though his civilian relationships do not compare to the level of connection that he felt with other military people, that this does not frustrate him. He still feels connected to civilians and can even confide in civilians about his deployment experience:

> There's nothing like your war buddies. . . . I've always believed, and we talk about training which is another thing which there's a difference. So, like, [my

girlfriend] knows some, but I never tell her anything that she doesn't need to know. Like what happens in Afghanistan is like conversations I'd have with my good army friends, like people who can relate to it. There's no point in worrying people who weren't there. There's no point, like, you need to—the biggest thing people need to do is like what happens in Afghanistan, Iraq, can't stay there—you can talk about it. But you need to talk about it with people who can relate to you. Everybody's got mates from the military that they can get up and talk about it with but . . . people need to understand that there's lots of people, you have people to talk to. You know? There're spots out there where you can talk and get help.

Again, this veteran is aware of the difference between civilians and military, but he does not hold civilians accountable or feel that they have failed him in their lack of understanding about combat. He is able to compartmentalize in a healthy way and find a relation in the way that he needs to. Similar to the Norwegian veteran above, he takes the difference between military and civilians to be one of circumstance rather than character.

One account that was closer to American veterans was a Canadian veteran who was candid and fatalistic about the possibility that civilian relationships would ever compare in strength and solidarity to those connections he had with the members of his military unit. However, he clearly recognizes that it is valuable to temper one's idealism and standards when setting expectations for civilian relationships:

To me, [civilians are] strictly only work type relationship, it's not that I don't talk to them. I talk to them, I consider them coworkers and friends, but I don't feel the same connection that I felt with my platoon mates, that connection simply isn't there. I still get along with my coworkers and we do things together but it's totally not the same. . . . At first it was excruciating, to put it the best way, it was so difficult to make the transition while I was still transitioning. What made things worse was that I would be in classrooms with a lot of people because my undergrad was in Political science and my graduate was in the same so my seminars were about international relations things that we would talk about the conflict in Iraq and Afghanistan. It took a long time for me to adjust to where I am now so it was really frustrating. It definitely is frustrating because I wish it was an avenue where I could still maintain the type of relationship that I had with my platoon mates and transpose that to the current job with my coworkers. It would be so ideal, but I understand the reality of not living in a perfect world.

Clearly, there were frustrations in the reintegration process for this veteran. These frustrations resonate with the sentiments expressed by American participants. However, similar to other NATO allies, the frustrations do not linger, and this veteran is intentional about his desire to reconfigure his identity and close the gap of social distance between himself and his civilian peers.

A part of what makes reintegration difficult for any veteran is the distance between someone who has experienced combat and someone who has not. Being exposed to the atrocities of war can be isolating because it is traumatic, but also because it is a side of reality that many will never have access to. This creates a very real gap between military and civilians even in a supportive culture. Another Canadian veteran explains this in the following way:

> It was kind of a roller coaster of emotions, I know early on it was extremely hard especially social gatherings. It's really hard to reintegrate especially with people that haven't seen the ugliness that's out there in the world. It's really hard to find things in common with people that haven't experienced a lot of things within war. Then a lot of it is that I have a little social group of friends that are super supportive, it just took a lot of time to rebuild myself back to where I was comfortable in little groups. Now, it's usually I need to know an exit strategy, but the integration was definitely a roller coaster that started off pretty intense but has subsided over the years.

This veteran was deeply affected by a traumatic experience and major physical injury in Afghanistan (he was hit and significantly injured by a rocket propelled grenade in a combat ambush). Among other effects, trauma affected his sense of connectedness with civilians and emotional stability in social interactions. He admits that he thinks it is incredibly difficult to have a shared sense of experience with individuals who have not experienced war. However, what makes this expression unique is that, despite his awareness that civilians cannot fully understand his experience, he still wants to form connections with them even if he has to be mindful of his limitations.

Perhaps in part because they tended to see the differences to be because of circumstance rather than character, NATO ally veterans were much more willing to take responsibility for their end of the reintegration process. If there was a disconnection in American veteran's experience, this was wholly the fault of civilians and their lack of understanding of combat. NATO allies were much more likely to take some responsibility for their disconnection. For example, a German veteran explains the complications involved in staying in connection with his family, friends, and relatives while on deployment:

> Maybe this is a personal thing, personally for me, I think it's important to stay connected during my mission to my relatives, family, friends, whatever. Because what I did, I really did a deep dive into that mission, yeah? I arrived

> in Afghanistan and I had the feeling my life ends and this is my new life. And I committed 100%. I felt a very strong responsibility for the life of my soldiers, I wanted to be 100% focused. But this on the other hand, as I said, every two or three weeks I did my home calls. And they were, it's tough to say, but they were not really important to me. I took them because I had the feeling that it's important for them and that's why I did it. For me it would be okay to be happier there, I don't know. But now that I came back, I realized okay this disconnection feeling is also a little bit my fault.

As the commander of his combat infantry company, this veteran needed to commit incredible amount of attention, detail, and care to approximately 150 soldiers entering combat. Though he did make sacrifices in prioritizing the mission for his troops, he also felt a social and moral compulsion to stay connected to his civilian loved ones. Whether he fully succeeded in staying connected to his loved ones while deployed is not necessarily the point. He wanted these connections, desired to keep them strong while deployed, and desired reconnection and reconciliation when he returned. The desire to stay connected and the ability to see that disconnection is something that is reified by both civilians and military could be critical in closing the social chasm between veterans and civilians in the reintegration process.

Returning to an idea that we discussed in chapter 1, it is important to understand that this is not merely a matter of individual choice and action. American military members are much more physically separated from civilians from the very beginning of training as compared to our NATO allies. This is relevant because it might make a connection and the desire for it erodes early on. Active duty American servicemembers are required to undergo a permanent change of duty station, on average, every 36 months of service. This leads to multiple moves throughout the duration of their careers, and though servicemembers can put in requests for location, depending on rank and need, these requests are determined at the division level far removed from the servicemembers requesting. Beyond this, the sheer geographical conditions of America combined with the strategic decisions on where to place military bases make it so that some or the most densely populated areas of the country don't have active bases for hundreds of miles while some less densely populated cities and towns are basically taken over by military bases. All in all, this makes it difficult, if not impossible, for American servicemembers to stay in close contact with their family members throughout the duration of their active duty contracts. This sense of physical distance from civilians that begins in training and continues for the entirety of the military career clearly has an impact on the sense of social isolation and skepticism that many American veterans have toward civilians at the end of a military career.

## A CASE STUDY IN SOLIDARITY: ISRAEL

In many ways, the Israeli experience of both deployment and reintegration is radically different from other NATO ally countries. The rates of PTSD in the Israeli military are strikingly low compared to those of American servicemembers despite the fact that both of these nations have been active in the war on terror for the past two decades. The most obvious difference between the two countries is mandatory conscription. In Israel, all citizens are enlisted in the military at the age of eighteen unless they apply for a disability waiver. Therefore, the ratio of citizens who have served in the military to those who have not is quite small. This fact makes Israel uniquely positioned to show how the synchrony between the Israeli military and Israeli civilian culture might affect the sense of solidarity that Israeli servicemembers would feel with Israeli civilians.

It is worth noting at the outset that the cultural differences were so vast between Israel and America that it was difficult to explain the struggle that Americans have upon reintegration. Many of the issues that veterans face in America are simply not present in Israel at all. Perhaps unsurprisingly, the most striking difference in reintegration was the experience of solidarity with civilians. There was even a bit of curiosity and surprise that we would inquire into whether there was a gap in solidarity between Israeli servicemembers and Israeli civilians. When asked about a disconnection with civilians, an Israeli veteran said this:

> No. Well, yes and no. First thing first, all units are really different. So, one specific unit doesn't know what the other unit does exactly. But then generally no, so that's why no because it's a really small country and everyone has this awareness of this military service. And everyone knows the units more or less. They know which units are more important and which are less and generally what the unit does. So, if for example I tell a story of my experience in the army to some other Israeli, he will understand completely what I am talking about. We have a common point, you know. It's not something that one percent of the population does. It's like more than 90 percent of the population goes to the army. And the ones that aren't whether with their medical conditions which not permitted them to go or they don't want because of illness, I don't know. But it's something that is common, and I didn't feel like people didn't understand me because of what I did.

It is important to note here that this veteran was a servicemember in the Israeli Army's special operations community during his service tenure. Similar to America, these are the most elite combat units in the Israeli military. Their selection processes, training processes, and combat missions are incredibly stressful, challenging, and, ultimately, unique. And yet, serving as a member of one of the most elite special operations units in the world does not cause him to feel misunderstood or detached from civilians. As he mentions, everyone takes a different job and the service itself is always a space for common ground for Israeli citizens.

At the time of the interview, Israeli #1 was studying to become a doctor and was a premedical undergraduate student at a major university in another country in Europe. During the interview, we decided to press further with the participant, asking him about his relationships with college students to see whether there might be a gap in solidarity there. We probed on this matter because so many American and some NATO ally participants had already expressed so much disdain for and frustration with college students and their perceived sense of naivete toward the world. When we asked this veteran about the disconnection that he might feel at school, he reported quite the opposite:

> No, no. I'm not feeling disconnected. In fact, I live with my girlfriend there, she's Israeli also, there are also like others in (European country) so I have some Israeli friends that know me a little bit better. And I like to say that I went to the army I did that and that but people react to that to in a way that is really interested and they don't look at it as something, it isn't beautiful. It's not beautiful that we have an army we're doing it for survival, let's say. But still it's something special and people are really interested in it.

It is important to note that even while studying and living in a foreign country where there is no conscription, little admiration for the military, little social capital for service, and an incredibly small population of servicemembers per capita, this veteran *still* feels connected to the civilian college students he encounters every day. He even acknowledges that being in the army isn't, in his words, "beautiful." In his estimation, it is not a job that deserves extra levels of glorification. It is a necessary job that must be done, and while he was proud to take up his portion of the service demands, it is not an element of his life that seems to dominate his identity and social interactions.

Of course, much more research is required for understanding the effects of mandatory service on social reintegration for veterans, and it is beyond the scope of this project. However, it seems likely that mandatory conscription alleviates much, if not all, of the disconnection that veterans feel when they return from deployment. The shared national experience makes one's perception of the service less unique and, thus, less likely to dominate one's social interactions after service.

## CONCLUSION

In this chapter, we have explored solidarity as a barrier to reintegration for both American veterans and NATO allies. What we found was that almost all servicemembers across cultures report feeling a truly unique kind of camaraderie and solidarity with the servicemembers in their platoon. Training and serving with people under extreme stress is a connective experience that is simply not often repeated elsewhere. This, in itself, did not seem to be what caused problems with reintegration.

We also found that American veterans seem to uniquely struggle with solidarity in two ways. First, the intensity of the disconnect with civilians is much more intense in America than in our NATO ally countries. The second was the duration of that disconnect. While some NATO ally veterans reported a similar disconnect, it seemed to be temporary rather than lasting and based on miscommunication rather than character flaws. NATO ally veterans were disappointed that civilians could not seem to understand their experience, but they did not extend this to all civilians. American veterans had a much bleaker and fatalistic view of civilians in general.

We explored this difference in a couple of ways. One of the most interesting, and indeed chilling, was the presence of true disdain or hatred for civilians that was present in American veterans. We found that the root of this disdain and hatred was in the training process—which could explain why veterans who have not deployed still feel disconnected with their civilian counterparts. Another was the way that NATO ally veterans seemed willing to fight to regain a sense of solidarity with civilians. This meant taking some shared responsibility for the disconnect, and also having a much less permanent, character-based view of civilians.

Also striking were the ways that NATO allies did cope and find solidarity with civilians. We found three common threads to this process: acceptance that some civilians simply cannot understand what it is like to serve and deploy, next some forgiveness of that, and finally the willingness to take some responsibility for the civilian/military divide.

Finally, we examined Israel as a case study in solidarity. Since Israel is a country that has mandatory conscription, nearly all citizens serve in the military in some capacity. This increased civilian fluency about what it means to serve—even in elite special forces positions—accordingly decreased the feeling of disconnection. Indeed, the questions about feeling disconnected were often met with confusion and curiosity because the idea seemed so foreign. This seems to suggest two things—one, that mandatory conscription and/or increased literacy about what it means to serve would naturally decrease feelings of isolation and disconnection, and two, that the presence of a civilian/

military divide in the culture of any country is a crucial factor in determining whether the reintegration process will be successful.

What is especially hopeful in this analysis is the fact that reintegration need not be as difficult as it sometimes is, and that war need not be an experience that forever dooms one to isolation.

## *Chapter 4*

# Idealism, Shame, and Aggrandizement

In the previous chapters, we have unpacked the differences that we found between American and NATO ally veterans and hinted at some of the sources of these differences. Since it is undoubtedly the case that American veterans struggle with reintegration in a way that NATO ally veterans simply do not, it is worth thinking about the sources of this struggle further. In this chapter, we will point to three tendencies in American veterans that revealed themselves in our research. These are tendencies that seem to have an important role in both the origin of the struggle and the lasting nature of the struggle.

The first is idealism shame, which is our term for the lasting shame that veterans feel when they have not lived up to the idealistic expectations of military service. As discussed in chapter 1 on training dynamics, veterans often go to combat with unrealistic expectations of themselves, of what combat will look like, and of the mission to be completed. Leaving for service with these expectations and coming home without having met them creates a lasting sense of insecurity and failure.

The second is aggrandizement of service, which is when veterans falsely report either fragments of their deployment experience or their military service on the whole, or both. The exaggeration of what combat was like, or the extent of one's service, is tied directly to idealism shame. In the absence of tangible success, veterans are compelled to create success milestones for themselves as an attempt to close the gap between expectation and reality. This creates a toxic dynamic where the veteran is attempting to gain accolades for things that he knows he did not do. The dynamic is especially toxic because if the accolades are not gained, the veteran feels as if his own feeling of failure is being justified by society. If the accolades are gained, the veteran knows that they are based on falsified reports of his experience. Either outcome further solidifies the idea that the veteran has a right to be insecure and ashamed.

The third is entitlement. When we asked veterans about training and deployment experience as an attempt to understand the military/civilian divide, we noticed a disturbing trend among American veterans—there was a strong thread of disdain and even hatred for citizens. As we showed in the previous chapters, this sense of disdain and hatred begins in training, and then continues throughout service as American servicemembers serve and protect civilians that are completely detached from military life. This is further complicated by the fact that servicemembers are falsely promised social capital for their service. The social capital turns out to be worthless, which provides another reason for disdain and hatred for citizens and significantly complicated the reintegration process.

It is important to emphasize that we are not blaming veterans for the difficulties that they face as they reintegrate. Rather, we are presenting a complex interlocking set of systems that prevent healthy reintegration, which both creates and prolongs trauma. If we want to truly understand what makes the American reintegration process distinct and more difficult than NATO ally countries, we have to examine the role of each system involved. A part of this system is the veteran himself—but it is important to note that the identity of the veteran is at least partially constituted by these systems.

## IDEALISM AND SHAME

An American veteran was especially candid about the kind of social conditioning present in training, and how this pertains to idealism. According to this veteran, the possibility of the perfect soldier is offered up as a standard to soldiers during training and throughout their careers. Pointed examples of courage, valor, and flawless performance are also constantly used to motivate servicemembers while on deployment. Throughout his reintegration process—which was lengthy and punctuated with painful experiences—this veteran came to understand that he was not grappling with trauma in the way that we expect veterans to. Rather than being disturbed by the atrocities at war, this veteran was haunted by his failure to live up to the ideals that he had woven through his identity as a solider:

> My implosion stems from these overwhelming feelings of guilt and failure from my time overseas. I felt worthless. I felt like a failure and would dwell on, over and over and over, like a film real in my head. I would project it into the future—if this situation presents itself again, how would I have been able to deal with it differently. . . . I would have anxiety over (my mistakes) for

> days and the only way to get rid of that was through more medication, more substance . . . it was a self-feeding cycle. It all goes back to those feelings of guilt and failure.

This veteran went on to talk about how the mission in the Iraq and Afghanistan wars was impossible to finish—the war on terror is not a battle that can be fought and ended. Fighting against an idea was something that made it very difficult to close the door on his past experience.

There are many other American accounts that explain this pervasive feeling of idealism and inadequacy. The veteran below explains how, even among military peers, there is a kind of competition among servicemembers who are deployed that centers around whether they experienced combat firsthand:

> I mean you take your half percent of the one percent of the population and then you break it down even further to the amount of people who have actually been in direct action and conflict and actually squeezed the trigger. I think the last time I did the math on it or saw the number it was something like 30–40 thousand people living in the United States have actually fired a shot at an enemy.

This veteran goes on to describe how this sense of singularity and, consequently, insecurity among those who may not have fought in combat became pervasive when discussing his initial entry training as an ROTC cadet:

> Some veterans when they come home because there's all these other combat veterans that they can go to for support, but the veterans that really didn't do much they can't connect with the combat veterans and they don't want to connect with the civilians so they are just on their own. . . . In ROTC I had a cadre who was eighteen and a half years SF, was a ranger and did everything you can do and we are all just sitting there like, "We are never gonna be this guy." It leads to a lot of people to lie about their service records. . . . And you get all these alpha male types who wanna be the best at everything they do and they don't see the military as just a job, it's a lifestyle. If they can't be the best, and it's very clear all the time with all these people they talk to and people who have done more honorable services than them, it's just gonna keep breeding feelings of inadequacy. Like the guy that was SF and platoon cadre, he didn't wear anything on his uniform. That almost makes it worse, when you're trying so hard to compensate for something and you got this guy walking around with no ranger tab, no airborne school, just a green beret and you know he's done everything, that gotta make you feel even more inadequate because you gotta address the fact that you're compensating. We have this AG officer walking around every day with his combat action badge showing that off and then Sergeant Whitehead just walks around with his green beret and we are just like, "Okay how many

> guys has this guy killed?" The SF guys, they are just at the top of the totem pole in the military hierarchy.

The participant here describes in detail how, from the initial phases of his training process with the Army, a pervasive atmosphere of inadequacy was being conditioned into young cadets. It is not as if the participant expresses any explicit or intentional culture of building this sense of inadequacy. There is no claim that ROTC instructors are saying anything to shame cadets during the training process. Nevertheless, the participant experiences an atmosphere—one that resonates with his ROTC peers, as well—of inadequacy and insecurity before he is even commissioned as a lieutenant.

Another American describes a unique and somewhat bizarre tendency in American military culture while individuals are in deployment settings. He explains how, while in theater, it was common to witness or hear stories of American servicemembers being dropped into potentially dangerous terrain for brief periods of time in order to gather combat action experience:

> I knew a couple of guys that when they were in Iraq there was a place that they were stationed in that became known as "Cap Valley" because you would get these insurgents out there who would take pop-shots at the patrol from six hundred meters out every day. Nobody would ever get hit but you were pretty much guaranteed contact if you went out on patrol with no real threat. So they would helicopter out these high-ranking officers out there who had never gotten a combat action badge and then they would for just twenty minutes out on their patrol for when someone actually there for a year sitting there watching it and being like "this is disgusting." Even when we train, when we run, we are singing about killing, in free time we are talking about killing, and then when we get deployed to Iraq you don't get a chance to kill anyone or see combat and then you feel like your service is lesser than the people that did get to do that.

There is perhaps no behavior that is as representative and symbolic a symptom of the precise nature of toxic idealism than this. It is important to note that these servicemembers are not being dropped into "Cap Valley" to actually fight the enemy. Though there is no reason to doubt that they would be prepared to fight if they were attacked, the very nature of "Cap Valley" allows for a sense of security despite some proximity to the enemy. In fact, there is nothing even relevant to mission completion or troop welfare at place in these drop patrols. What is being described in this passage is reckless behavior fueled by the desire to get recognition. Implicit here is a kind of structure where "real" combat has to be experienced for one to be a legitimate servicemember. Ironically, there is nothing sacrificial or service-like about this behavior, even though its aim is to meet that ideal. It is worth noting that not only were NATO allies often more cautious in their approach to enemy engagement, but there were no accounts offered of NATO servicemembers intentionally being dropped into a potentially dangerous circumstance only to receive a combat action badge or an extra ribbon for their dress uniform. This points to the pervasiveness of the idealizing of combat and hero worship present in American military culture.

This veteran continues, explaining what he believes to be the etiology of this tendency in American servicemembers:

> I think a lot of it is insecurity. More than anything I would just blame the way veterans compete with each other. Comparing who has their ranger tab, or their combat action badge, who has been in longer, what deployment. I see all these veterans shitting on each other saying Kuwait isn't a deployment. It's kind of shitty. And the hierarchy within the military really promotes this insecurity. Cadets for example in ROTC are at the bottom of the totem pole. Everyone universally hates them, and you'll find that every cadet knows that. They aren't even butter bars yet. So they shit on other branches and civilians but everyone else in the military still hates them. When I was in ROTC, we would talk shit about the Air Force ROTC because they stayed in hotels and inside to do their training. Marines refer to themselves as the "men's department of the Navy." It's one of those things that start as good nature and then no one realizes when it's gone too far and then it's just taken way too seriously. When you get a lot of alpha male types, in a career like this there's gonna be a lot of this competition and people actually measuring dicks with each other and comparing who's done more. Then so many people have gone through this all, done their part and they still feel inadequate.

Another American speaks candidly in this passage about how an environment of good-spirited competition can quickly turn into conditioning of inadequacy and showmanship. What manifests as a competitive ribbing may be rooted in a deeper level of insecurity, shame, and destructive idealism among servicemembers. Hierarchies are essential in military service. However, there is a major difference in separating enlisted and commissioned servicemembers and what is described here. When these hierarchies become a constant assessment tool in order to ascertain who has more credibility and legitimacy in their service, this reifies feelings of inadequacy and shame.

## AGGRANDIZEMENT

It is somewhat unsurprising that these specific and relentless ideals of combat that are present throughout one's military career could result in aggrandizement, or the exaggeration of one's service. If one is trying to meet an impossible ideal and cannot, a way to resolve at least some of this tension is to make it look as if one did meet the ideal. An American veteran describes this in the following way:

> I just feel that those people who have been through that (combat), get much more support than the people that didn't do anything but wanted to because they can't identify with anyone. It's almost like people who don't deploy or face combat while deployed feel shame behind their military service. It's interesting the way that veterans and people in the military get to lie. It's subtle. They lie using people's assumptions. My buddy in the Marines hasn't done anything but when he talks to a civilian he can say "I was in the marine corps infantry, was a sniper, and deployed four times." And civilians know better than to ask if they've killed anyone or seen combat because that's rude. But he can just say those things that are all true and everyone's just gonna assume that he's been in combat and killed people and that's just gonna make up for the inadequacy.

There are several aspects of this description worth mentioning. First, the veteran describes that the ability of American veterans to aggrandize service records is tied inextricably to the contact and culture gap between American civilian culture and American military culture. Simply put, American veterans can aggrandize their records because American civilians wouldn't have the knowledge, criterion, or wherewithal to actually engage in critical questioning toward American veterans. Second, he provides an assessment of servicemembers who have less experience and less combat exposure than their peers. American MV describes how some servicemembers can manipulate the idealist and naive assumptions of American civilians to exaggerate their service records and engage in showmanship and self-aggrandizement toward civilian peers. Finally, it is not the lying, per se, that is concerning here. Instead, it is the reason why American veterans might feel prone to exaggerate their deployment experiences and/or combat exposure and how the act of lying might increase shame and detachment from civilians.

The aggrandizement of service, also referred to as stolen valor, allows individuals to live up to the idealized fantasy of military service, as well as the perceived expectation of significant social capital offered in American culture for military service. Though no participants in this study offered descriptions of their own personal tendency to aggrandize service, they spoke of the behavior as common in American military culture among their peers. It is possible that these accounts of exaggeration are themselves exaggerated by American veterans. Though we have reason to believe that is not the case, what is most relevant is the way that the aggrandizement of service records speaks of a social and cultural phenomenon that is present in American military culture.

An American veteran described how he experienced the aggrandizement of service records after returning from multiple deployments to Iraq and Afghanistan. He offers multiple accounts of this phenomenon during his military career and in his return to civilian life and encounters with other veterans:

> A lot of times, (veterans) aren't accountable to anyone. In the military, I remember I was walking by this kid one day and he had just gotten off shift, like an army police patrol shift on the base and he was like a private, and he looked to another private and was like, "Yeah, I shot a dog on patrol today." I instantly looked around and was like, "You didn't shoot a dog today." He was like, "What?" I said, "You didn't shoot a dog today. If you discharged your weapon, you would still be at the MT station being investigated." He was like, "Well, I didn't shoot a dog, but I thought about it." It's like that sort of thing, or there is no accountability. People can self-aggrandize as much as they want because most people didn't deploy with them, so they don't know if the stories they told were true. I used to hear ridiculous stories all the time. Most of the time I'd be like, "Yeah, yeah, okay. Whatever." It is kinda like the loudest person in the room has done the least amount in their life. Unfortunately, that's other veterans that are just like, "Oh yeah, I did this and I did that." There is another guy that I went to college with. He was one of those people who was really loud and telling all these crazy stories, all this crazy stuff that happened in the military and I would just be like, "Oh my god, dude." It got to the point where I would stop calling him out on stuff because I didn't need to. I knew when he was BS'ing. I was like, it's not hard to see. And they just go with it. College students around them, they don't have the credibility to call veterans out on it. But I have met dudes, and I'll be like, "Why did you join" and they say, "I just wanna kill people" and those are the dudes who just make shit up. . . . It might be one of those things that the military makes you feel like you are a very special individual cause like you made it in. Like, out of all the civilians, we chose you and you passed every test and then you beat combat and you are amazing. And then they get out and this is where I, this is what I honestly tell people. I'm like, "Listen, no one is special." We are all the same, we are all people. We are all just trying our best. A lot of people don't wanna hear that. Especially in the military.

This veteran continues and draws connections between hero worship and the tendency to aggrandize one's experience.

> I think it is prevalent and I do think it is an issue and I think it's not just with MOS combat, it's our whole society. We have this hero ideal of everyone in

uniform, like my wife jokes with me because I hate wearing my uniform to go anywhere. . . . People will come up and grab you and touch you and shake your hand and hug you and stuff and they are like "Thank you, thank you for your service." I'm like, "I'm paid for this service is and volunteering." I'm getting paid, I get to go to college for free, you know? To me (the military) was like a job. It's interesting to go see combat but that's part of it, I knew what I was signing up for it's not like it's a surprise. It's not like "Oh no, I have to go to combat?" Like nah, I joined when two wars were going on. I knew what was happening, but I do believe that our society has this big issue with making heroes out of pretty much anyone who served and like it does go to a lot of people heads. And then they could get out and they have a very inflated idea of importance and ego. Some of the guys get out and are like "Yeah, if I go to a job and they offer me less then 70k a year I'm turning it down." I'm like bud you better hope you start at 35 or 40, if you get a degree.

For this veteran, the experience of such a hero ideal became somewhat of an absurdity. There was a constant juxtaposition between his own intentions to serve and a culture of hero worship that he witnessed as pervasive among his peers. In this, he witnessed a perpetuation of self-aggrandizement and almost delusional thinking in many of his younger peers who were exiting their active duty contracts. His own realist attitude toward service and a career after service was likely able to protect him from such tendencies. However, he is able to lay out in this lengthy passage what potentially deleterious effects were in store for those who got swept up in the culture of hero worship.

He continues and describes an account of how another younger veteran with less experience was almost subconsciously aggrandizing the narrative accounts of his peers as he attempted to put together a diary of veterans' experiences:

They feel the need to justify, and I definitely think to validate, to make it real. I think there is so much judgment against those, type-A-ers, ya know? It's like you can't show weakness, you don't want to show weakness. But at the same time, you want your symptoms to be acknowledged as real. I got a good friend of mine. He's one of those young guys that when he got out, that's all he knew. He was only in for a couple of years but that was his identity. He started doing journaling and interviewing guys who went into the Marine Corps and all that's what he was doing, he was embellishing stories, so all kinds of shit. I was like, "(Friend), I can't participate. You either tell what happened or just write it yourself. Don't be interviewing the guys. You're messing with fire. You're interviewing the guys, you're adding your own little twist on it, like you were there and stuff. If you're gonna tell the story, tell it the right way." He ended up dropping the entire project. He said I was right.

By all accounts and measures, this young veteran's intentions were sincere and noble. He was attempting to bring the stories of veterans to civilians and perhaps even bridge this knowledge gap. However, despite any sincere intentions, the tendency to aggrandize their records and his own in these stories worked its way into the narrative until he was called out for it.

American JK continues, describing how the etiology of much of this exaggerating and aggrandizing of service records was likely tied to the severely competitive nature of the American military, even within military companies who were performing the same mission:

> There was this competitive part though. 'Cause we were heroes, so it was like, let's just go all out and tell a big story. There was a sibling rivalry that existed through my entire unit. Even my company bravo level, half of it was on the west side of the valley, my platoon was on the east side of the valley. Our whole AO was a mountain range on the east, and the rest of the company was west. The west was getting beat up most of the time. They lost the most guys, so I think the guys on my side especially felt a little shadowed. They were living in the shadow of the rest of the company. But that existed at the battalion level too, the other companies would get jealous of us, the bravo company, which had its own little rivalry within. You go up and up and up. It's not just the civilians in the military, it's the military in the military. It's wild.

He is describing a ubiquitous process of comparison and evaluation among his peers across different companies and battalions fighting, for all intents and purposes, the same mission. On its surface, it can be confounding to think that companies and battalions who were seeing less combat were actually jealous of those that were taking on heavy enemy contact and higher casualty rates. However, when considered within the context of both this sense of idealism—what a servicemember's mission *should* look like—and the severe level of showmanship between units and personnel, one can see how envy can fester between servicemembers. It was not as if his unit asked to be on the safer side of the mountain. To the contrary, they wish they could have had the more dangerous mission. Their inability to get that mission really might have come down to nothing more than drawing of straws at the battalion level and likely had nothing to do with a personal evaluation of their ability or inability to fight the enemy successfully. Regardless, they feel a sense of inferiority as a result of this lack of mission—the same sense of inferiority that other companies and battalions feel toward them in the endless quest to position oneself in the pecking order or military pride.

He continues, ultimately offering his suggestion for servicemembers who come back and may feel a sense of inferiority and the need to aggrandize their service:

> I think the lack of braggadocio is key (for a healthier transition). It's too easy to fall into a habit, if that becomes a routine, you're fucked. It's funny about the infantry, you're halfway. You're not a pencil pusher, you're not a badass but you're somewhere in the middle. That's where all the braggadocio bullshit comes into the mix.

This American veteran returns to this theme of competition and showmanship in the American military as the psychosocial etiology of this "braggadocio bullshit" he sees among some of his American veteran peers. Curiously, he mentions how it is often this middle ground—being high on the military social capital food chain but not quite at the top of it—might lead servicemembers to aggrandize their records and bring them closer to those whom they perceive as "above" them. Again, what is presented here is the infinite regress of measuring one's worth against all other service records. Simply put, there are no victors here. There will always be some veteran whose experiences outweigh one's own; there will always be a bigger "badass" than you. In this case, though infantry is likely on top of the social capital food chain compared to almost all other MOS's in the military, they still are not special operators. If a veteran or servicemember cannot remove himself or herself from this infinite regress by reexamining their own intentionality and reorient toward greater intrinsic motivations for service, this perpetual sense of insecurity and self-aggrandizement will never be broken.

Another American veteran describes how American servicemembers might be tempted to manipulate the social capital tied to self-aggrandizement of one's service record upon returning to civilian life. In addition, he addresses how the complicated layers of shame and social currency surrounding narratives of service in America might make many American veterans simply stop sharing their story with anyone, including other American veterans:

> I think very few people are joining because of social capital—but I think that they capitalize on that afterwards. I think they're joining to get money for college, good health care, stability—those things that are less and less accessible to the middle class these days. And when you're telling about these genuine, terrible experiences that you have—having someone sitting there trying to one up you—"Oh, but I did this thing"—which you know didn't really happen, but nobody else there knows either. It just makes you not want to discuss it at all with anybody.

As mentioned earlier in the book, social isolation and the perceived lack of connection to American civilians are known stressors for American veterans who are struggling with reintegration. However, in this passage, we see a potential etiological factor contributing to the tendency from veterans to not share their experiences with anyone—other veterans included—when they return. It is difficult to imagine a more negative response to someone's attempt to confide a trauma narrative than to immediately one-up their story. This competitive and evaluative tendency is fundamentally dismissive of the individual's experience of trauma. It is possible that so many veterans are suffering in silence simply because they fear that their stories will be one-upped and negated by other real or exaggerate accounts of trauma offered by their veteran peers. Though the sense of distance from civilians and civilian culture is certainly a factor as well, the American military culture of braggadocio, showmanship, and exaggeration can quite likely be contributing to the silent suffering of many veterans, as well. This veteran continues:

> I think these young men and women that we send to fight our wars either drink the Kool Aid or they don't. What I mean by that is you're either bound to the whole thing or you aren't. I also think a lot of it has to do with the fact that our current culture is one that everyone is looking for a reason for something to be wrong. I think it's more difficult for people to just accept that sometimes simple shitty things happen. Sometimes we just have to deal with it and push through, but I think everyone's just looking for something, ya know? A bigger reason for why they are suffering.

In other words, given current American culture, the simplicity of one's combat experience, combined with the trauma or suffering they carry from this experience, might be leading servicemembers to exaggerate their accounts. Instead of just accepting that combat, deployment, and trauma can be devastating in their simplicity, veterans might look for a way to embellish the account in order to justify its effects. Furthermore, he explains how these explanations of suffering can themselves become a form of competition among veterans—a suffering Olympics of sorts. Tying this back to the concept of toxic idealism, in the absence of achievements that map onto our outdated conception of combat, veterans are left to advocate for their own validation. Instead of competing based on who achieved the most or who completed the most missions, tasks, etc., the rewards are tied to the quantity and quality of pain endured. These rewards are epitomized in narratives rather than badges or medals of honor. Recognizable trauma narratives become the measuring stick—a kind of perverse social currency.

An American veteran describes how this sense of idealism is affected by the way both American military and American civilian culture engage in a form of hero worship around combat service and enemy engagement in combat. He describes how this perceived sense of heroism is likely to contribute to building a social gap between veterans and civilians:

> We are going to have to stop seeing every soldier as a hero before both the lying and any connection between the military and civilians comes to pass. Unfortunately, that is not the popular view. The nationalists may come after you when you publish this.

This description reveals some of the pervasive cultural mindsets that likely contribute to this sense of idealism in American veterans. The tendency to aggrandize one's service or engage in stolen valor is only possible in a culture that engages in this form of hero worship toward military service. It is interesting that without prompting, this veteran explicitly refers to the aggrandizement that American veterans are tempted to engage in and ties it directly to this cultural idealism—as he puts it, hero worship—of military service.

As mentioned previously, when the actuality of one's service record is placed in juxtaposition to this idealism, there can be a sense of shame and insecurity formed in the conscience of the servicemember. Again, even for American veterans who deployed to Iraq or Afghanistan, the overwhelming majority were not engaging in active fire fights or even experiencing any level of enemy contact. Though there is certainly something heroic about performing one's support mission with honor, integrity, and focus while deployed, this form of a deployment experience is wildly different than what many in American culture might perceive about a deployment experience, especially when American culture is so far removed from the day-to-day inner workings of these wars. A human resources specialist in Afghanistan has tremendous responsibility, but little to none of it involves actively or personally fighting the Taliban. The vast majority of these military jobs are not epitomized in movies like *The Lone Survivor*, *American Sniper*, or *The Hurt Locker*. Yet, it is possible that the majority of Americans reduce their understanding of military service to those stereotypes. This cultural mindset may lead the American veteran to exaggerate his or her own service record to live up to this ideal. Perhaps even worse, this tendency may cause one to feel a deep sense of shame around such hero worship for their service. Finally, it may lead American veterans to view civilian work and civilian service jobs as a lesser form of service than military service.

## LACK OF IDEALISM, SHAME, AND AGGRANDIZEMENT IN NATO ALLIES

The form of idealism and hero worship described above was found to be quite unique to American culture in this study. One of the major insights in this research is that this sense of military service holding some singular uniqueness or carrying extra social capital of being tied to heroic was relatively unique to American culture and, thus, American veterans.

Distinct from Americans, almost all of the NATO allies interviewed for this project explicitly expressed that military service was no greater or worse than any other form of civil service that a citizen might engage in. Rather than have a set of ideals about military service, they simply saw serving in the military as one of the many possible ways to serve one's country. A British veteran expresses this in the following way:

> There are for sure other [forms of service other than military] that are just as important and necessary as the military. Especially for police and NHS, they do a great job. I don't feel like the UK or civilians owe me anything, it was my choice to sign up. I don't feel like anyone owes me anything.

This veteran very clearly recognizes the value of other forms of service to society as equivalent to his military service. Given what we can see in the mindset of the American veteran, it is difficult to imagine Americans, veterans or civilians, equally acknowledging the value of military veterans and Medicaid doctors, for example.

Another British veteran acknowledges that he felt a sense of pride and self-aggrandizement, especially after passing all of his early entry training. Nevertheless, like most themes discussed in this book, though NATO allies' experiences are on the spectrum of what American veterans describe and may experience, the way this phenomenon is described does not appear to be nearly as severe, socially isolating, or functionally impairing for NATO allies as it might be for American veterans.

> So the first six weeks you wear attire, kind of like the Americans wear—like the caps, you know the caps I mean? Our patrol caps. We used to wear them for 6 weeks, yeah? And then if you passed your sixth week, then you are allowed to wear your maroon beret with a big green badge behind it to show you're a recruit. So, after week 20, if you passed P-company, the green patching comes out and our maroon berets could get like a wings patch. So, when you ask if I felt different from civilians when I got back from training with my maroon beret, I felt like I was a boss and that I was above every civilian. That was really short lived though. After that, I just remember feeling like I achieved. Hardly anyone achieves. Because when we start training, like by the time we got to P-company, it started with like 60 and it was 11 of us left. But no, I didn't feel detached from my friends, family, or civilians as a result. I was just proud of what I had achieved.

This veteran has a sense of personal accomplishment for his efforts in completing special forces selection. However, such an accomplishment in British culture is largely unrecognized in comparison to American culture. Navy SEALS and Green Berets in America have taken on an almost celebrity-like status in the American cultural psyche.

A British veteran expresses how he does not perceive his choice to serve and deploy to Afghanistan as worthy of any significant extra value to his civilian peers:

> No one comes around my house and says to me, "(Participant), we need you to join the military and go to Afghanistan." No one coerced me to do that. I approached them and then joined. It would be different if I was going to WWII and I'd come back and everyone was like, "Oh I know why you went to fight." No one made me fight. That's the way I see it. There's more good than bad in the world and you need to just enjoy it. There's so much good stuff, so why waste your time getting annoyed about something that's really not worth your time. You should be happy in yourself. No one asked you to go, you wanted to go no matter what you've done inside.
>
> Worrying about what civilians understand or don't is just a stressful way to live. Someone will say, "Afghanistan was absolutely pointless." And you think, "Well, did you go to Afghanistan?" And they go "Oh, I never did." At that point you just laugh and walk away. You went and did something there, whether it's right or wrong, you did something there. I can stand there and I can go, "You didn't go. You don't know." But what's the point of that? You're building your stress, your anxiety, everything up for nothing. The bloke will never remember he said it. This is where you have a choice to face it stuff like that. Someone annoys you, instead of arguing back, just take a breath and just turn around and walk away. . . . In the special forces, you deploy a lot. My mates and I on deployment, we are all good. I don't know, you get paid a lot of money to deploy, so I made my choices.

This veteran clearly acknowledges that it can be frustrating to hear someone speak ill of the war in Afghanistan if they did not deploy or serve. However, his reaction is tempered down from that of the American veterans. He reiterates throughout that his service was his choice and no one else's. The sense of autonomy and responsibility he feels around his service allows him to perceive military service as probably little more than a different career choice.

It is worth noting that NATO ally veterans were aware of the trends that we are pointing out with American veterans. A British veteran addresses some of the perceived differences between American culture and British culture on how military service is viewed from a macro-cultural perspective.

> See your country has a very, very different demeanor around military service. Your whole American rigor, you know, you need to join up, you need to do this

> for your country—it's not like that in the U.K. It really isn't. People really think, you know, you're an idiot for doing that. You want to go to war? You know people aren't like what you're saying in the U.K.

What this veteran is describing is the perceived sense of social capital tied to military service in American culture that is likely lacking or absent in British culture. As mentioned in the earlier analysis of this section, the perceived amount of social capital offered in military service cannot be overstated as a significant factor affecting a perceived sense of idealism, pride, and distance from civilians. Whether or not American culture offers tangible social capital to American veterans—a topic deeply worthy of its own discussion—a perceived sense of social capital can form a sense of social cognition that entitles one to a sense of esteem and dignity from his or her peers after leaving active duty. This can undoubtedly make it difficult for an individual with such perceived social capital to take seriously the opinions of his or her peers. On the other hand, in British culture, this same perceived sense of social capital appears to be limited if not vacant. It is clear that NATO ally veterans didn't expect to be seen as a hero for their service, nor did they expect to be seen as a fool for signing up to go to war. It is possible that this mindset worked to temper expectations of civilian encounters when reintegrating to civilian society.

A Canadian veteran described his experiences both in the Canadian military and with American civilians and veterans, which have formed his perspective on just how destructive a mindset of idealism and consequent social isolation can be for American veterans. He describes what it is like to witness these juxtapositions between American culture and Canadian culture in their praising and support of military service:

> My wife is American and last March, I went down to (American city). Yeah like I'm a stone's throw from the border. I've met American veterans down around there at the county fair or at raves and it's like, yeah, okay, you served years ago. Good for you. Time for you to shelf that. You're not gonna move forward otherwise and they go to college with that mentality. They ostracize themselves from other students and they end up failing. They have such an attitude of entitlement and such an attitude of "I'm better than you" and they hold on to their service so much that they're never going to be able to move forward. They live in the past.
>
> I think it's like this veteran lifestyle, the black rifle coffee and the grunt style shirts and all different you know, like, "Good for you. We're veterans. But shelf it, man. Integrate. Come back to the world. You're not in anymore. Leave it where it was." The difference is they hold on to the difference. They take pride in it, even, and it fuels them and motivates them and I'm like, "Hey buddy, that is totally dysfunctional, like that's not good for your brain. You're not gonna grow." Being a veteran isn't a job or a lifestyle. Being a veteran is a part of who

> you are, like let it be a part of you. Be proud of it but for the love of God, it's in the past. Time to move forward.

This Canadian veteran clearly understands temporarily struggling with reintegration and coming back to civilian life. However, he speaks directly to the lasting struggle that seems to uniquely face American veterans. He sees this overattachment to one's military identity as a way of refusing to move forward, of holding the distance between military and civilian life. It is also interesting to note that according to these accounts, it is not the lack of social support that is harming American veterans as they navigate life after military service. Instead, it is the desire to hold deeply to military identity as a way of separating oneself from civilians and aggrandizing one's stature that is most deeply affecting veterans as they transition from active duty.

A German veteran offered a nuanced perspective on the sense of honor and dignity he feels toward his service in Afghanistan. He acknowledges both the sense of pride and distance from civilians and the deep need to resist that sentiment in civilian life:

> The thing is that I never get the feeling that I do what I do for Germany somehow. I just did the dirty job and when I came back, I wasn't only proud I was. I had this feeling being superior to others. Having done something very dangerous and very adventurous. Something very special, but not for Germany, as I said there's this feeling that I or the atmosphere that I saw in 2010 which was paratroopers who said we don't care about Germany, we don't care about our families, we do our own thing here. Now this is a feeling that I had more or less. I think when I came back, I was a little bit arrogant. And I was running around and arrogant and the thing is about being arrogant is no one cares. If you are so proud of something and no one cares like okay this does not work. And I don't know why, I don't want it to be like that, but it was just in a feeling that I thought about it, it was just the way it was. And after a while I realized that this is something which is not normal. This is wrong in a way so this is one that does not work actually so let's see if you can make society interested or caring in a different way. Because this mindset does not work. Coming back, being arrogant and hoping that everyone else thinks that you are a hero does not work, at least not in Germany. Now, I don't have the feeling that I did more than other Germans for our country or something. But I just think that we did a dirty job and parliament sent us so people should care in a way just not treating us as whoever but just showing interest. Not even respected just wanted them to know. Just to know what we're doing. That would have been enough.

This veteran candidly acknowledges a similar sense of pride and dignity that he felt upon returning from what he so aptly described as the dirty job that no one else wanted to do. He continues, describing the effect that this sense of pride and entitlement took on his personal relationships:

> I felt it personally because my former girlfriend was the one who had to experience that phase. It was not easy for her. And now looking back, I was even arrogant towards her, yeah? What is she, what is her responsibility? I mean she just wanted to be nice and I was so arrogant. I acted like king of the world that . . . I don't know. We are not together anymore of course. One thing is, I mean, now knowing what can happen, I know from the beginning how not to behave. So, I learned from that experience, of course. Obviously, there is a gap. You call it a gap. There is a gap between what we do and what others think that we do. And I would, from the beginning, and I think that makes you a little arrogant somehow, like, you have this special experience and you feel like superior in a way.

This passage succinctly and aptly describes the sense of empowerment and nobility one might feel when returning from war. What is unique here though is the conscious wrestling with this sense as this veteran reintegrates. There is a palpable sense of awareness, guilt, and regret about these feelings that resonates in this passage—this kind of awareness was nowhere to be found in American accounts. Despite the presence of such behavior and antisocial attitudes toward German civilians and even his loved ones, this German veteran ultimately expresses a unique sense of awareness of how destructive this mindset can be. Perhaps it is impossible to not feel some significant degree of pride in the aftermath of military accomplishment. Nevertheless, further research should go into what builds this pride to the point that it becomes such a self-destructive and antisocial hubris, as well as whether certain training protocols can be followed to temper this and build greater self-awareness.

## FALLEN HEROES: VICTIMHOOD AND ENTITLEMENT

Tied to both idealism shame and aggrandizement is a tendency to feel entitled to certain tangible benefits, acknowledgment, and social capital upon reintegration. This manifested as identifying with victimhood, as well as grasping tight to pathology as a way of gaining potential benefits and entitlements from systems in American culture that support disability. Consider the following three American veteran accounts:

American 1:

> I think that sometimes guys will blow it out of proportion. The reality of it. I think that guys who are trying to get benefits from the military. Let's say they have a symptom, I hope this doesn't come off the wrong way but,

> their symptoms will manifest because they are trying to get something for it. That sounds terrible and I'm not phrasing it right but, honestly, it is fucking true.

American 2:

> A lot of vets come back entitled—having the army be your first job outside of your home. It has problems because on a day-to-day level you're actually just not working at the level that most modern places require. And, so, some of the vets I've run into are spoiled little sons of bitches that don't put out the effort that civilians do. I mean, you're going to run into the cultural narrative that is so hard because the narrative is that once you put on a uniform and serve your country, you're a hero of freedom and you're worthy. But that's not the way it is. It doesn't actually change who you are. But people grab right on to that meal ticket with both hands.

American 3:

> I mean, I think there is a few different reasons for [the high rates of PTSD in America]. Number one is money, they get money from the VA. If you claim PTSD enough, in your little sessions, I have read a bunch of articles about this. I know it is a thing. Like, I know people who do this. I am not going to go rat them out to the VA, because I don't want them to get caught.

The judgment present in these accounts is striking. The second American suggests that American veterans are not willing to put in the time and effort required to succeed in civilian careers. Though this is certainly possible, it may also be that certain aspects of active duty military life make it difficult for American veterans to adjust to some of the demands of civilian life. For instance, the vast majority of active duty servicemembers in America have tremendous administrative support around things like food, housing, finance, healthcare, childcare, and education, among others. This type of structured guidance and/or bureaucratic support is simply difficult, if not impossible, to replicate in civilian life and the civilian workforce. Furthermore, many jobs in the military involve very clear, consistent, and specific work routines, as well as an unambiguous management culture. It is not difficult to imagine that American civilian careers that involve more independence and less structure being justifiably difficult for some veterans to adjust to.

The third American's analysis is quite a bit more straightforward. He claims to know veterans who simply feign symptoms of PTSD in order to receive greater disability benefits. Though this explanation might appear on its surface a gross exaggeration, there are reasons to support its validity. Due to the lack of biomarkers in diagnosing PTSD as well as the documented evidence that the department of Veteran's Affairs was and is understaffed and, thus, overwhelmed by PTSD claims from veterans of the wars in Iraq and Afghanistan, it is not difficult to surmise this a system ripe for malignance and manipulation. Considering these factors in conjunction with both the lack of perceived support offered by American civilians and the sense of psychological entitlement that might be conditioned in veterans from the culture of idealism and self-aggrandizement we discussed previously, at minimum, more research should be devoted to the quantity of malignance that might exist in these claims.

Another American describes how the intersection of sacrifice, social isolation, and the sense of valorized patriotism displayed in American culture toward military service all work to build a sense of entitlement in some American veterans:

> You started asking yourself questions like, "Why am I doing this and the other 99.2% are not doing it?" I would say that's a feeling we ourselves or maybe society has created. Like a feeling of entitlement, how much we think we as soldiers that we are entitled to. How much value or what is the cost of my time in Afghanistan. Like, how could you repay that? A $50,000 per year job, would that be enough? Would you give me 4 years of free education? And that's an answer that I don't have yet. Now I can tell you that based on my cultural and ethnic background, I can tell you that having the ability to go to school free—well, in some sense free—is something I value. You know, I went to Afghanistan, now I get my education. But that might be a problem, like how much entitlement we think we should get? It's time you'll never get back, especially when you've been in combat and you have those memories that you can't erase. You were mentally healthy, and you came back, and how much of your mind and your brain and your mind cost—that's a good question.

This veteran addresses several factors that are worth emphasizing here. First, he rightly points out that the wars in Iraq and Afghanistan are likely the first time in history that the profound burden of fighting in two theaters of war for close to two decades of time has fallen upon less than one-half of 1 percent of a population. War has always existed, but societies traditionally send a larger percentage of their population to fight. This sense of social isolation in the theater of war is unprecedented in modern history. After multiple tours in theater, it is natural to begin to wonder why other able-bodied young adults are not fighting alongside you.

Second, this veteran grew up in a poor working-class family in Puerto Rico and alludes to the fact that the military paying for his extensive college and graduate education—he was working on his second master's degree at the time of the project—might seem like a fair trade-off despite his multiple deployments. Nevertheless, he also expresses the curious nature of human desire and the complex reality that all too often the more one gets the more one feels is deserved, perhaps especially in light of such an immense sacrifice.

Finally, at other parts in the interview, this veteran does describe the extensive amount of trauma and moral injury he experienced while deployed. Though he did get mostly free college education and healthcare benefits, he also spent years in therapy processing the horrors he was exposed to. He finishes this passage by reminding us that there simply may be no price one can put on the experience of trauma. In some cases, perhaps it is this level of trauma exposure that leaves veterans feeling like they deserve more when they return to civilian life in America.

Another American veteran discusses the way that victimhood can become a kind of identity for some veterans when they return to civilian life:

> Like, if I suddenly got PTSD, that's going to create a new identity for me as a veteran and that's a victim veteran. That's an easy thing to fall into. That's being like oh I been a victim of these terrible circumstances that I put myself in, and like I don't have to do anything about this. It's funny because, and I could go on more about if you want, is the problem of the military's inability to teach most soldiers how to handle this type of mindset. That goes back to the entitlement like, "Oh, I served. I was deployed. I should get everything." I tell people this, to me it doesn't make a difference. You can get PTSD from a car accident. You can get PTSD from somebody hitting you in the head with a baseball bat. You don't have to go to combat. Unfortunately, the prevalence of you seeing something or being involved in something is so much higher in combat situations but a lot of people are like, " Yeah, I have PTSD because like a sniper shot me in the face, I have PTSD from that." No I don't. But I don't have PTSD because I had different expectations and a different view.

This American participant is candid here, expressing his own personal combat trauma—being shot in the face by a sniper—but explaining how such trauma did not cause any extended symptoms of PTSD. Ultimately, in his estimation, it is not just combat trauma that causes such severe PTSD in veterans. Instead, it is when one believes that one's experience of combat trauma is singularly unique from all other forms of trauma that the difficulties faced with adjustment to civilian life are deeply compounded. Such a myopic view of one's personal trauma over all other forms of trauma leads to a sense of social isolation and identity foreclosure that make it just as hard for social reintegration after service.

Another American describes how, in his estimation, this mindset of entitlement and victimhood has slowly eroded a more original sense of motivation to service resulting from the desire to sacrifice and honor one's country:

> I never heard any leaders ever talk about any sort of privilege that comes with wearing the uniform or leaving the military. Like, you get paid to do what we tell you to do and we're telling you that all these people are paying your check at the end of the day and you joining to protect them when they can't for whatever reason and chose not to, so you need to be that selfless person. I don't know how it's gone from that and what you're taught while you're into all of this complete polar opposite. Like, I deserve everything because I served my country. Honestly, I just think that in the veteran's stance right now. Suicide is just popular. Like it's a cool thing almost in just a weird way. We put up this thing saying we don't want to lose our brothers. But at the same time, we talk about how depressed we are. I feel like they just like being a part of the cool club. Being traumatized, depressed, suicidal, mistreated or being misunderstood. It's kind of just like this cool club.

Admittedly, we were hesitant to even add this passage to the analysis. This description comes across as an extreme and reductionist assessment of suicidality in the American military community. Such hasty assessments might lead to unfair stigmatization and victim shaming. There are at least a few important points in this passage worth analyzing. First, he describes the possibility that there is what he describes as a culture of depression in the military. What is expressed here is a sentiment expressed by many participants that American veterans might take a perverse sense of pride in being perceived as dysfunctional and surly. Secondly, he points out how there is a dichotomy between higher-level military jargon on suicide and the on-the-ground lived experience of embracing such tendencies among veterans. Despite the lofty ideals preached by battalion commanders and the countless drill halls across America plastered with suicide awareness brochures, posters, and paraphernalia, the lived experience of American military culture might actually be one that fosters and romanticizes an archetype of personal brokenness.

Another American veteran echoed this idea that some American veterans might find themselves embracing a diagnostic label of PTSD because it validates their sacrifice.

> We look at PTSD and its labeled and scrutinized and we have soldiers who will casually rattle off they have PTSD in front of other soldiers, and I will say it's kind of strange. To some people, it sounds like an honor to say they have PTSD. I think our military is very different than in many other countries I've seen, especially in the tendency to almost embrace this label of being traumatized. It is almost like this dick measuring contest is affecting men and women when they come back. Yea I mean, I don't have a stack, you got medals, AIB, Pathfinder. I think we are the only military that I have seen that wears all that stuff on their regular uniforms every day. Imagine if you went on a college

> campus and all the professors were wearing their publications on their suit coats. That would be ridiculous. But how could you not feel inferior? It's difficult for me to validate my service to people who don't understand what we really do. But for family friends and people who have served, I don't have that problem. But especially people in the ranks, if I went to a new unit, it would be endless questions.

Corresponding with the previous sections in this chapter, this American articulates the role that showmanship, competition, and self-aggrandizement in American military culture play in creating this tendency in American veterans. Just as one's uniform ribbons, combat, and school tabs tangibly demonstrate one's worthiness in garrison culture, perhaps one's diagnosis of PTSD more tangibly justifies his or her deployment experiences. Bearing the signature wound of combat becomes the ultimate proof that you sacrificed sufficiently.

Finally, in a similar vein to these accounts, this last American veteran describes how he believes that many American veterans are actively seeking to be labeled and diagnosed with a psychopathology.

> Everyone wants a diagnosis. Why? Disability man. That's a huge incentive. We are incentivizing mental health problems. There's a huge difference between recognizing and helping them, I think. It's complicated. . . .The cultural incentivization of war trauma as well as the financial benefits. I don't think people are like honestly going, "Oh I need a diagnosis so I can go on disability so I'm going to play the game." I don't think necessarily that's happening a lot, but I think that we've just made it cool to be a damaged soldier and . . . I don't know. I feel like the cultural incentivization is a part of that. Because, look, I mean, that's what's different. That cultural narrative—that's what is different between us and our allies. I think that the overall cultural narrative [in America] is just so pressurized. I think that something like mandatory service would change the narrative and changing the narrative is extremely valuable. Like I couldn't—without knowing all the other effects—I don't know if I could recommend mandatory service. But I feel like changing the narrative is important somehow. It would make it so that everyone else at the table could say, "shut the fuck up" when someone starts talking about their PTSD that's not even real. Unfortunately, it's like the welfare thing. People need the help, but if you start talking about how people are faking it for welfare than welfare goes away. I wish you all the luck trying to explain this side of it. I have no idea how you could possibly say that in our culture right now.

Similar to other accounts, this veteran alludes to the tangible entitlement benefits veterans are allotted from disability claims. However, his argument goes further as he expresses both that outright malignance is probably quite rare and that there is a sociocultural form of capital that comes with a PTSD diagnosis. In his perception, because so many American civilians have little to no contact with American military culture, the nature of military work, and the atmosphere of deployments, it is wildly easy to exaggerate one's deployment narrative and trauma experience. If there was less a chasm between civilian and military culture in America, civilians would be keener to such exaggerations and, thus, veterans might be less prone to do it.

Finally, this veteran is deeply concerned over how to even express this narrative in a nuanced yet candid manner. He laments how a small number of maligners could ruin the necessity of a welfare disability system for those truly injured and traumatized at war. We echo these sentiments. Despite how difficult it might be to read some of these passages that paint a more selfish and entitled portrait of some percentage of our veteran community, we must not overlook the reasons why we have come to treat these men and women as heroes among us, if only in idea. One challenge in painting the portrait of lived experience through qualitative research is to be able to hold contraposing concepts in the mind at the same time, allowing each to coexist in their right and engaging both with analytic openness, skepticism, and curiosity.

## Closing the Gap by Cutting the Pride

To end this chapter, we will offer a series of passages that involved participants describing what could be done to resolve this sense of idealism shame, aggrandizement, and entitlement in veteran populations. Solutions to curbing these tendencies were offered cross-culturally, involving ruminations from both Americans and NATO allies on this topic.

Earlier in the chapter, a German veteran described how he felt a sense of pride and entitlement that led to antisocial tendencies when he returned home from Afghanistan. Later in the interview, he describes what steps he took to curb these tendencies:

> If I could do it over, I would try from the beginning to close that gap by being transparent and authentic. For example, I would talk to journalists and send my reports home and write things and post stuff on social media right from the beginning. Like, to not let this disconnection start. Somewhere it starts, and I think it starts at the end of my training like when I came to Afghanistan, the disconnection started. I had a lot of pride after that and felt different from other people. If I could do it again, I would try to let that gap not take place from the beginning. As I said by just not let the relationship get out of sight, I don't know. It took me awhile to do this and start really telling my story, trusting people would understand it. Once I did, the feeling of disconnect slowed down.

This veteran pins the sense of social isolation he experienced between himself and German civilians to his own feeling of pride after his initial training leading up to his deployment to Afghanistan. Similar to the sentiments expressed by Americans, this German participant began to feel an inflated sense of ego and self-aggrandizement around his deployment to Afghanistan. He mentions how even in the ramp-up training he began to feel this sense of pride, speaking of the possibility that even servicemembers who do not deploy can experience a severe sense of social isolation. However, this sense of social isolation wore heavily on him and he began to take specific strides to bridge this gap and dissolve the sense of pride he felt. As described in chapter 3, he made efforts directed at building solidarity, empathy, and trust with German civilians through sharing his story with anyone willing to hear it.

An American continues this line of description, discussing how narrative accounts can help bridge this gap and reduce the sense of self-aggrandizement in veterans. He expresses how a more candid, simple, and straightforward description of war experiences helps in closing this gap:

> There is a lot of pride in the military. I'm not trying to say that I don't have that pride because, regardless of my personal feelings, our country uses young men and women for their benefit of the country over the individual with the boots on the ground . . . I mean, at the end of the day, there's nothing serious about it. War is work, ya know? I do think that anybody could have done it. Now with that being said, I think that you do need to have a processing psych eval. The things they do at MEPS is kind of horseshit. I think it could be better. I'm a firm believer in belief for service. I don't think everyone needs to go and pick up a rifle, but something, whether you're serving in the armed forces, public service-related, or health care, I think things like that would probably do better things for our country. I mean I think that I could be completely off on that too but. . . . No one is too good to bend their back in order to help someone else whether it's picking up a rifle or patching someone up.

This approach attempts to make changes both to deployment narratives and the idealized image of the servicemember at war. He begins by describing how the nature of the majority of military jobs are no more than support level forms of work that would be done at any civilian workplace (e.g., human resources, communications, personnel assessment, management, finance, logistics, healthcare, etc.). Even though this veteran was a combat arms veteran, he still does not perceive his own infantry job as anything more than work—no different than any other service job that takes endurance and sacrifice. He finishes by fully endorsing this leveling of the hierarchy, arguing that many Americans could have successfully done the work on a deployment and that many Americans do similar work in their everyday lives. It is worth noting just how radically different this mindset is to the sense of pride, aggrandizement, entitlement, and hierarchy expressed throughout this chapter.

Another American veteran echoes this sentiment:

> The work we did was just another job. There is no reason to feel this sense of pride over it. We did it well and I am proud of doing it well, but it was just a job and other Americans could have done it well too.

Finally, an American veteran describes how he transitioned from a combat infantry MOS while in active duty to a public affairs MOS in his National Guard unit:

> I am good with my job now. I know what I did in the past (serving in the infantry), but I don't really feel like what it is was special. Yes, a lot of other veterans, especially younger ones, looked at me that way but I never got into it for those reasons. I knew this was always just something I wanted to do. It's not service. I like being in the Army. I liked being in combat and now I like taking pictures for my unit. Both jobs matter.

This veteran had an incredibly unique career transition in the American Army. First, he successfully navigated from active duty service to the National Guard and very much found satisfaction in his Guard unit. It cannot be understated just how difficult of a transition this can be for active duty veterans. Just as there exists a hierarchy among branches and MOS's, there is undoubtedly a similar hierarchy between active duty servicemembers and reservists. The term "weekend warrior" is a commonly used nickname that is loaded with pride and degradation especially when one considers that a significant burden of the wars in Iraq and Afghanistan was shouldered by reservists and members of the Guard. Not only does this veteran navigate this transition to the Guard without any sense of pride or entitlement over his peers, but he takes a job that could not be further from his MOS in the infantry. The fact that he is completely at peace being the unit photographer in a National Guard unit after being a purple heart recipient in an active duty infantry unit cannot be overstated. His career transition and adaptation to civilian life (as an accountant) and reservist life (as a unit photographer) might be one of the most unique stories we have ever examined in our research with veterans. Ultimately, the point of this story is clear—such an unprecedentedly successful transition is tied directly to such an unprecedented level of humility and self-awareness in this participant.

## NATO Allies in America—Startled by the Adulation, Praise, and Entitlements for Americans

As mentioned previously, several NATO allies in this study had either lived in America or traveled to America at some point after they had completed or had a pause in their military service. This gives them a unique vantage point with which to experience their American counterparts after combat. What stood out to many of these participants was how much, at least in word, praise, adulation, and entitlements American veterans were given compared to NATO allies in their respective countries.

A German veteran who lived in America for several years after his initial entry training and service with the German military describes the cultural differences in the way the military is perceived in both societies:

> The biggest difference is certainly the kind of support that you at least believe soldiers get from society. Anecdotally that's totally different in Germany. Well I mean if you just drive on (the highway) and you have "Welcome Hero" signs. You read the newspaper and it says, "Our heroes in Iraq." *A soldier in Germany would never be called a hero by anyone for many reasons.* In Germany, the mere effect of you joined the armed services doesn't really mean that you're a hero but be it the entire political spectrum, I mean in the U.S. no one would criticize the military as much as they do in Germany. They do these studies and they come up with very positive numbers about what society thinks about the military. But then you have these other numbers, or you have this anecdotal evidence that no one really appreciates what the military does in Germany.

We intentionally emphasize the phrase in the middle of this passage because it appears to encapsulate the differences between German culture and American culture in its purview of military service. In German culture, military service is not valorized because the valorization of the military builds a fertile ground for autocratic nationalism and the justification of genocide. Germany's history is sensitive to the effects of unfettered nationalism and how it leads to a lack of serious and critical analysis of military usage and military behavior. In America, we have yet to fully feel the negative effects of patriotism in such a severe way. Outside of Vietnam, there has been and currently is very little criticism of the American military of the behavior of American veterans in civilian society. As described by this veteran, this hero worship is ubiquitous in American society and could not be more diametrically opposed to the mindset toward service in German culture.

A British veteran describes his perception of how military service is perceived in the UK. He expresses how rare it is for British civilians to honor and valorize the service of veterans and how few benefits British veterans receive compared to Americans:

> No one knows what goes on, especially in the U.K. The military, how it runs out in America, is equal and respectful. People just aren't as respectful (in Britain) as they are out here (in America). In the U.K., people look at military service

> as like you had just done this insane thing. Then you get back and then you just stood with normal people that couldn't give a dung that you were away. They don't appreciate or respect that. The military down here (in America), you get a lot of respect and you've got flags flying everywhere. It's not like that in the U.K. Such as a state building. There's no flags up or anything. Nothing that gives you a reason to fight.

While American veterans might feel that these outward displays of solidarity are essentially empty, it is important to note that in other countries these displays simply do not exist at all. The patriotism in America is much more explicit than it is in other countries. This veteran went on to express his wish to have access to some of the help and acceptance that his American counterparts had:

> I feel like America is definitely where I should have been born a long time ago. Because you get help as well. When I left the military, there's programs that you get 6 months before you leave. The way they do it in the U.K. is you get 4 years, then off 3 years, then the last year you hand in your notice or you stay in a one-year rolling contract. And on your last year, the last six months is your resettlement states and the military will give you one month and give you 500 pounds which is probably about $700 to do a course without books what they recognize. So, I didn't use that because of various other reasons. Then you get 3,500 pounds which has to be used within three years of leaving the military to use on a registered course again. Then you have to pay 25–70 yourself. So, I just moved out (to America) and I emailed (the British VA) asking if I could use it out here because I live in America now. They said no. They said I have to use it in the U.K. Then I started seeing things out here from the patrons like the U.S. Marines we were training with. The support your soldiers receive once they leave, the G.I. bill, I can hardly believe it.

This perception that American veterans have it easy when it comes to social support is certainly a rarely articulated opinion. We asked this veteran for more details and wondered how he might square his perception of the relative ease of being an American veteran with the astronomically high suicide rates:

> So, I'll tell you something, right? I'd tell you I remember his name but when I was in California taking a parachuting course, I met a U.S. Marine. It's not somebody who I know, it's someone who I met. I was just talking to him, he had just left the U.S. and he said that before he left, he told them that he had like a medical injury so he got a pension or payout each month for the rest of his life—there's nothing wrong with it. He spoke to me and went on about it. Yeah, and sometimes I was wondering, is it too much? It's almost like if you

> don't get (the benefits), someone else will just get it. So why not just take it? At first, I was like, well, that's not right! That's more looked down upon in my country. He was like, "You should do it before it's too late." I was like, "Well, we don't get that." You get something if you get hurt, but not something you can sort of just make up. You Americans get a lot, don't you? So maybe if you get a lot, you want more?

This veteran is careful in his assessment of how the differences between British and American civilian culture and their attitudes toward military service differ. He also describes the effects that these differences are likely to have on veterans in each culture. First, he mentions how in Britain, there is little to no social capital in serving. Second, he describes how the social welfare entitlements American veterans receive are far greater than in the UK. He describes his college experience to that of his American peers with a fully funded G.I. Bill to explain the difference. Finally, he echoes a similar sentiment from the previous description, explaining how so much entitlement might lead a deeper longing for more benefits instead of having the effect of proportionate gratitude.

Another British veteran describes what it was like to be welcomed home by British civilians after a deployment, comparing his experience to what he witnessed when American veterans returned home from deployments:

> I didn't find it to upset me as much, but I certainly noticed a difference here between the US and the UK. We had done multiple training trips in the US with them and as soon as we landed at the airport you guys were greeting us and like everyone was super proud of the military and I liked that. In the UK its very town dependent, I guess. My town is famous for its Navy and Marines and stuff so a lot of people are on our sides and can appreciate it. But then you can go to other places and they're very left-wing and hate everything—And, like, I'm still getting military discount in some places over in America. We don't have the GI Bill! If I had fought for America and done the same exact thing I did in Afghanistan for America then I would be going to college for free right now. We get these free workshops to help you write a CV and stuff but after working with Americans we had a few friends who were in the SEAL teams and they were like, "I got my pilot license and my helicopters license and I didn't pay for it." And, yes, obviously they're at the spearhead of your military so yeah, they're gonna get looked after more. The UK does a pretty poor job on that.

Like the other participants in this section, this veteran realizes that the level of military support in British culture is different from that in America. Interesting, before the interview for this research, this veteran was misinformed about the distribution of G.I. benefits in America. He presumed that special forces veterans went to college for free because they were "the spearhead of your military" in Afghanistan and, thus, they receive excellent benefits for their service. As logical of a presumption this might be, it simply is not the case. Save for enlistment bonuses, the American military offers the same level of benefits to all active duty veterans who complete their contracts with an honorable discharge. Whether one has completed multiple deployments, one deployment, or no deployments, whether one was involved in heavy combat or whether one never left the forward operating base, all G.I. eligible benefits are distributed equally to American veterans.

Our final passage in this section comes from a German veteran who lived in America while he pursued a graduate degree when he was a junior officer in the German military. He describes what he perceived as a stark contrast in the level of public support between German and American civilian culture toward military service:

> The thing is, yeah, the public support that can be seen in the United States is quite high. I studied in America and, of course, from time to time we wore our uniforms and it was great, yeah? Every five minutes someone says, "Thank you for your service." But then I remember a special situation at the Empire State building where we came there with our uniforms. We were just waiting in line and if you ever walk across the tower you can see how long you have to wait. And it was about three and a half hours. And we thought okay, "Let's go up there and let's wait." Then we realized how the people in front of us got nervous in a way and then after a while somebody ran out of the building and said, "Hey, you are soldiers. Come here." We passed by the whole line and we were the first ones who could use the elevator and go up to the Empire State building. It was great. And the thing is, in the line, no one was staring at us or gave us the feeling of okay this is not fair or something. It was like it was okay with them for us to cut in line. I had the feeling they would start into an applause every second. That was the atmosphere. It was so great, but I mean I was just a first lieutenant. I didn't do a lot of things for the army at that time, but it still felt great. It felt great. So, these things in the United States are very visible. But on the other hand, this is the one part, yeah? On the other hand, this is what you are doing. The veteran's associations and all of the homelessness, the suicides, etc. When it comes to these facts, publicly, everyone says, "Okay our army, our military, our firefighters, our policemen, blah, blah, blah." But when it's about money or really caring then I think it's another thing then.

This veteran offers several penetrating insights into both the contrast between German and American cultural attitudes toward the military, as well as the conflicting attitudes toward veterans within American culture. First, in German culture, regardless of wearing a military uniform, this behavior of cutting the long line would have been selfish and unfair. There simply would be no allocations offered to veterans while waiting in line because military service is not treated as a greater or more worthy form of service than any other career. Secondly, within American culture, German #2 perceived an irony in the way Americans offer verbal praise and modest entitlements (e.g., cutting a line, being clapped for at a sporting event, military discounts, etc.) with the larger systemic failure to fully empathize and support American veterans in their return home (e.g., homelessness, unemployment, suicide, etc.). This clash around support—between what is offered in word and praise with what falls short in larger sacrifice and empathy—quite possibly plays a significant factor in causing disorientation, social weariness, and cognitive dissonance for reintegrating American veterans.

What ties all of these reports together is the perception that NATO ally veterans have of what it might be like to be an American veteran. It should be emphasized again that these are all veterans who have firsthand experience living in America, so it is not the case that they are simply speculating from afar. They acknowledge the differences between cultures with near envy, while simultaneously showing awareness for the struggles that American veterans face as they reintegrate.

# Conclusion

What we have done in this chapter is to give a gloss of the interlocking ideologies that operate together and form significant barriers for Americans when they are facing the reintegration process. While previous chapters aimed to detail the different experiences that shape veteran experiences for American servicemembers and NATO ally servicemembers as an attempt to trace the struggle, the goal of this chapter was to highlight the ideologies and tendencies that we found to be unique to the American veterans that we interviewed.

The three tendencies we examined are idealism shame, the feeling of failure post-deployment that seems quite unique to American servicemembers; aggrandizement of service, the tendency to exaggerate and even falsely report one's service; and entitlement, the feeling that the veteran is owed something upon returning home. It is important to again note that these are interlocking ideologies that spring from one another. Were it not for the toxic idealism that servicemembers are shaped by from the very beginning of training, there might not be such prevalent aggrandizement of one's service record. If veterans were not made to feel that they had to live up to expectations of heroism, they might not feel as if they were entitled to tangible benefits as well as social currency.

It is important to again emphasize that we are not blaming veterans for the difficulties that they face as they reintegrate. Rather, we are reporting data that we gathered that may hint at some sources of the shockingly high rates of PTSD and suicide in American veterans. If it is the case that entitlement or aggrandizement exist on a large scale, as this research suggests, this is not because these individual veterans are entitled and self-aggrandizing. Rather, the systems that train and employ these people have problematic—and in many cases simply outdated—ideologies that prevent growth and instead promote stagnation. The systems of power that regulate the veteran are the same systems that partially constitute his identity. If there is to be change, it *must* be systemic.

## EPILOGUE

We were inspired to begin this work when we became aware of the stark differences in PTSD diagnoses and in suicide rates between American veterans and our NATO allies in the Iraq and Afghanistan wars. While we had spent a considerable amount of time researching the reintegration process, our research had been restricted to American veterans only. We wondered whether a cross-cultural analysis would yield a deeper understanding of the roots of the lasting and often fatal trauma that plagues American veterans. Our goal was to compare the experiences of our NATO ally veterans with those of American veterans in order to see if there were clear trends that might help us understand what was happening within American culture to make the reintegration process uniquely difficult.

One of the things that became abundantly clear right away was the presence of a deep divide between military and civilian cultures in American society. Perhaps better described as an abyss, there is a strong feeling that civilians and military members are fundamentally different and that there is nothing that can be done to bridge the gap between the two. While there was a varying amount of disconnect between military and civilian lives in all countries that we interviewed, it was starkly clear in American culture. This thread is interwoven through all of the rest of the research and therefore provides a central area for more research.

We began by examining the training process in these countries and we found that it is here where the military/civilian divide begins in American military members. This divide is deepened as civilians are established as "other" and military members are geographically separated from their friends and family for prolonged periods of time even before deployment. Also present during the training process for Americans were several other ideological trends that become problematic during reintegration. During training, the stage was set for toxic idealism, hero worship, and expectations of combat.

The identity of the servicemember was the topic of chapter 2. Here we found that there were three trends that American military members experienced uniquely. The first was what we have termed identity constriction—which is the experience of reducing one's identity entirely to a singular facet of it, one's status as a servicemember. Identity expansion—the experience of combat and service as expanding or enhancing one's identity—was something that many NATO ally veterans experienced but was not available to many American veterans. The last was identity coercion—which was when the military attempted to coerce servicemembers to stay, and treated them negatively if they did not. This resulted in veterans feeling less stable about their decisions. On the whole, American veterans experience a constriction or fragmentation of their identity—something that primes the veteran for reintegration struggle.

In chapter 3, we examined the experience of solidarity both with other military members and civilians. While we were aware that solidarity is at the center of the reintegration process, we found that American veterans seem to struggle with solidarity in two unique ways. First, there is an intensity to the disconnect with civilians that bordered on disdain or hatred sometimes. This is no doubt exacerbated by the existence of such a strong civilian/military divide and compounded by the experience in training. The compounding of these issues seemed to create the second unique struggle, which was the intractable nature of that disconnect. While many NATO ally veterans reported a similar disconnect, it seemed to be temporary rather than lasting.

Chapter 4 attempted to tackle three controversial tendencies that we could not ignore in our data. These tendencies were the idealism shame that comes from not being able to live up to idealized notions of combat, aggrandizing one's service as an attempt to close the gap between expectation of combat and reality, and a sense of entitlement that haunts American veterans and alienates them from civilians.

Ultimately, we suggest that the gap between American veterans and American civilians is widening. The lack of empathy and true attunement to the lived experience of military life and culture, combined with the expectation by American veterans that this respect, honor, and understanding will exist, likely leads to the tendencies described above.

It is critical to note that much of the struggle with coming home after war begins in the training process. Much of the struggle is directly related to the toxic idealism that servicemembers are exposed to from the very beginning of the training process. The idealism conditioned in American servicemembers, combined with the intense military/civilian divide, can lead to a motivation to never openly express vulnerability or suffering, especially to civilians. Unfortunately, the effect of such idealism manifests as an ineffective mode of repression. The irony of such repression is that it likely manifests as a deep sensitivity to any criticism from others, especially, again, from civilians. Precisely what servicemembers were trained to be resilient in the face—struggle—might be difficult to process in the face of idealism and the repression of vulnerability. Any civilian who has a critical opinion of the veteran who is repressing vulnerability is likely to be met with a more severe level of disdain and, perhaps, more volatile emotional or antisocial responses.

Each of these takeaways is worthy of deeper examination, further research, and theory testing. Nevertheless, even after examining the data and literature around these stark differences in PTSD and suicide rates between American and NATO veterans from OEF and OIF, we continue to be plagued by two questions. First, why do American veterans have such high expectations of American civilians? Having been civilians before their military service, it seems like it would not be such a stretch to imagine having a naïve understanding of what it is like to serve. However, American veterans seem to have a fixed belief that civilians should understand more deeply and also that they never could understand. This continues any isolation that the veteran might have felt and makes reintegration quite difficult. The second question is, why do American veterans have such high expectations of themselves? We believe that it is important to inquire into whether there is another dangerous intersection for these factors built into the fabric of American culture. In short, we posit that there is a significant aspect of American civilian culture that is worth considering more seriously in understanding the difficulties American veterans face in coming back to civilian culture.

American culture in the last generation has rapidly moved to embrace neoliberal values of self-aggrandizement, personal accomplishment, and individual success as almost moral markers of one's worth in one's community and society at large. There are both implicit and explicit messages built into the fabric of American culture that promote the individual and self-promotion being above all else. Though perhaps latent, this message is ubiquitous in the lives of American children and becomes a bullhorn in the lives of American adolescents and young adults.

It is worth considering Erikson's (1950) stages of conflict resolution in conceptualizing the effects of such a message of personal achievement above all else in late childhood, adolescence, and early adulthood. At an incredibly salient time in the development of industriousness, Americans often promote a message directed at the fear of inferiority above all else. Children, adolescents, and young adults are qualitatively measured in our society: grades, athletic accomplishments, extracurricular prowess, and college acceptance at the forefront of this race to the top. Where you went to college is valued over questions of selflessness, commitment, and moral contribution; "where did you go to college?" versus "what do you want to contribute?" or "how you can serve your community?"

When these messages intersect with the fetishizing of military service as social capital in American culture, it is impossible to ignore the effects of shame and self-aggrandizement within the American military community. The American military now becomes just another avenue by which a young person can build this social capital and aggrandize the neoliberal self in a desire to "be all that they can be." We argue that this intersection, of both neoliberal self-aggrandizement and military service as social capital, is simply not as severe in the NATO ally countries. We believe more research should be devoted to understanding what effect this intersection is having on veterans as they both enter the military and, ultimately, transition out.

As was just alluded to, it is of deep value to consider and devote research to longitudinal inquiries that examine the motivations of young men and women for joining the military in the first place. This will indeed be a difficult task. There are so many recitable platitudes around the desire to serve in America that parsing through these with qualitative analysis will take analytic insight, innovation, and courage. Cutting to the point, it is of potential value to look at the role that one's conception of self-worth is before joining the military. Are individuals joining out of the intrinsic motivation to serve because they are young, able-bodied, and living in a nation at war? Is it the sense of adventure and combat exposure that draws the individual in? Are individuals joining for the very real and substantive social welfare benefits allotted to American veterans? Or is it possible that young men and women are joining because they experience a lack of self-worth in their civilian lives outside of the military? Does this lack of self-worth in civilian life intersect with the tangible social capital offered from military service? Whether this lack of self-worth in civilian life is due to trauma, neglect, social isolation, bullying, or any combination of these, what effect will the gaining of social capital via military service have on that young man or woman when they then go to exit military service?

Finally, we imagine it is possible that a critical reading of our analysis can present a substantive rebuttal to our main thesis from this project—that American veterans from the wars in Iraq and Afghanistan feel significantly more social isolation toward and disdain for civilians than do their NATO ally counterparts. One might feel inclined to inquire why American veterans even need to feel connected to civilian counterparts. We posit two reasons for this.

First, it is incredibly difficult to establish any stable sense of life satisfaction without strong interpersonal relationships. There is much research supporting the connection between interpersonal satisfaction and life satisfaction. Decades of social science have been clear in demonstrating that when human beings feel connected, understood, and engaged with a community, their level of happiness increases. On the other hand, when an individual experiences isolation, mistrust, and apathy toward one's peers, one's level of personal happiness decreases. As long as many veterans continue to feel so isolated and disconnected from American civilians, the foundations of depression, suicidality, and substance abuse will continue to be present for reintegrating veterans.

Second, American military members, not unlike law enforcement, education, and municipal workers, are, ultimately, public servants. The first oath of the duty for all servicemembers is service to protect the Constitution and the freedoms of the American people. This is the public service of the American military. To stand between America and her enemies so that the unique liberties American civilians have might be protected. Included in these liberties are the right to be critical of the military and the right to be apathetic about military service! Any discussion of whether it is noble, helpful, or even ethical for American civilians to be so apathetic and/or critical toward military service is simply a separate discussion. We posit that it is socially, culturally, and politically dangerous for the American military to feel such detachment from and disdain for their civilian counterparts. Ultimately, this form of social cognition might over time tear so deeply at the fabric of our society that American servicemembers begin to lose their north star of moral guidance regarding the true purpose of their service and work. As long as military service in America will hold so much social capital, if American servicemembers are not joining with the intention of service and, likewise, if the burdens of duty and service are not being consistently reinforced throughout the training process, it would be incredibly easy for young men and women who join to lose sight of this purpose. This growing chasm can lead to incredibly damaging consequences for both reintegrating servicemembers and American culture, at large.

In closing, this research project hopes to proffer a unique lens into the difficulties that American veterans from OEF and OIF might experience after their active duty service and deployment experiences. We hoped to begin accounting for the divergent statistics around suicide, PTSD, and other mental health diagnoses between American veterans and veterans from NATO ally countries who also served alongside Americans in Afghanistan. We do not posit that the themes presented in this book are the only factors accounting for the divergent data between these populations. In fact, there were several other themes that came out of our dataset that simply could not be addressed in the scope of this book but that we hope to address in future publications. This goes without saying that this is merely one inductive examination of the phenomenon with an *n* of forty participants. Much more is to be said about these difficulties; however, we do stand by these themes as a unique contribution to the conceptualization of this phenomenon. We look forward to further engaging in both quantitative and qualitative research to further investigate these theories.

Below, we proffer several solutions that might serve to bridge the social chasm between veterans and civilians, as well as mitigating the severe sense of identity and idealism formed in training and active duty environments.

1. *Shorter deployments*. One of the most startling aspects of the comparison between Americans and NATO allies fell in the area of time in theater. This was especially true for American Army soldiers whose average amount of time in theater could be, on average, from nine to fifteen months and in some cases eighteen months. This duration of time was

roughly two to four times longer than NATO allies. Save for the sheer amount of stress and pressure that such a lengthy deployment can accrue, the tendency to foreclose identity and feel detached from civilians is likely to be exacerbated by such factors.

2. *Opportunities to establish duty and training stations that are closer to one's civilian home more regularly.* Admittedly, such an adjustment is complicated and would involve a series of moving parts to accommodate. However, setting aside the idealism of such a request, there was a palpable difference between NATO allies who were almost always able to train and serve relatively close to their civilian homes versus American veterans who were often far removed, geographically speaking, from their homes for both training and service. Part of this is due to the fact that, save for Canada, America is geographically so much larger than every other nation in this study.
3. *Post-deployment "vacations."* The Israeli participant in this study described an incredibly unique post-deployment strategy employed by the Israeli military. At the end of one's service term in Israel, the servicemember is offered a form of paid leave for an extended period of time. The Israeli participant in this study described how he and his platoon members were able to travel through Asia for weeks before they returned for their out-processing from active duty service. He described how this trip offered him an opportunity to, as a young man, meet civilians from other cultures and countries and broaden his perspectives on the world. There was no pressure to rush back to civilian life. Time was taken to process one's experiences, broaden one's horizons, and do this within the context of unit solidarity. We believe that a more extended form of rest at the end of one's active duty contract would be deeply beneficial for American veterans, as well as NATO ally veterans.
4. *No more "up or out."* In the active duty American military, there is a perpetual requirement for servicemembers to advance in rank or get kicked out. This means that when officers and noncommissioned officers are up for promotion, they must achieve that promotion or be discharged from the military. Despite the glaring fact that this is a wildly unusual corporate assessment system, there are several problems that arise from the choice to employ such a highly competitive, comparative, and severe structure. First, it leads servicemembers to push constantly for symbolic and, at times, superficial accomplishments that look good on a board file but do not necessarily have a clear connection to professional development. Second, this leads servicemembers who are otherwise content and proficient in their position to feel that they must be "achieving more" at all times. In the military, unfortunately, this notion of "achieving more" is almost always tied to measurable, empirical, and symbolic markers

versus more qualitative measurements and interpersonal assessments. For example, an officer is almost never promoted because he has gained the trust and devotion of his or her subordinates. The officer's subordinates are never even consulted in the evaluation process. This most surely would cause an American military leader to constantly seek empirical and measurable markers that justify their performance and leadership qualities (sometimes referred to as "chasing an evaluation bullet"). This system may in fact lead to the discharge of good leaders and the promotion of, though motivated, self-absorbed leaders. Furthermore, this system is likely to cause the pervasive inferiority complex that we have discussed at length in this project.

To be clear, none of the NATO ally nations in this study have the same promotion system as the American military. All of the participants in this study from NATO ally nations were allowed to stay in the military at their current rank for an extended period of time without the need to be promoted by some otherwise arbitrary deadline.

5. *Less "uniform trophies."* If one is ever given the opportunity to serve in NATO environment, one of the most glaring differences between American servicemembers and NATO allies is noticed in the presentation of their uniforms. American servicemembers are allowed to wear far more of their personal accomplishments on their duty uniforms than NATO allies are. For American servicemembers, most of these accomplishments involve the completion of advanced schools or deployment awards. For the vast majority of NATO allies, there is little to none of these uniform markers. We are concerned about the type of motivational atmosphere that is promoted when servicemembers are chasing advanced schools in order to show their status to others, versus the lens of intrinsic motivation of attending skills to build proficiency and competence in one's job. Like the promotion scheme, this is likely to build greater inferiority complexes among American servicemembers that are less likely to exist in NATO allies. Many American servicemembers will perpetually feel that they simply have not accomplished enough in the eternal quest for more "trophies" to justify their service record.

In concluding, one Canadian participant really epitomizes the differences between NATO allies and Americans on the social side of this transition. All veterans interviewed in this study, across countries and cultures, miss the sense of solidarity they feel with their peers. Nevertheless, this loss of solidarity simply did not affect NATO allies to the level that it did to Americans:

*I:* Do you find yourself still missing being a member of a platoon to this day?
*P:* I do for sure.

*I:* Do you miss it to the point that it disrupts your functioning on a day-to-day basis or is it something you have made peace with and you know it's in the past. What effect does it have?

*P:* I look back on it fondly.

*I:* So, it doesn't affect your daily functioning?

*P:* Nope, not at all. I am grateful for my time but, ultimately, it was just something I did.

# References


Ahronheim, A. (2019). IDF: 57,277 veterans recognized as disabled, 5,000 suffer from PTSD. *The Jerusalem Post*. December 15, 2019.

Armenta, R. F., Rush, T., LeardMann, C. A., Millegan, J., Cooper, A., Hoge, C. W., & Millennium Cohort Study team (2018). Factors associated with persistent post-traumatic stress disorder among U.S. military service members and veterans. *BMC Psychiatry*, *18*(1), 48. https://doi.org/10.1186/s12888-018-1590-5.

Bandelow, B., Sher, L., Bunevicius, R., Hollander, E., Kasper, S., Zohar, J., MÖller, H.J. (2012). Guidelines for the pharmacological treatment of anxiety disorders, obsessive – compulsive disorder and posttraumatic stress disorder in primary care. *International Journal of Psychiatry in Clinical Practice* 16, 77–84.

Bergdahl, B. (2016). *Serial*. https://serialpodcast.org/season-two.

Beynon, S. (2020). After years of failure to end the crisis, veteran suicide takes center stage on Capitol Hill. *Stars and Stripes*. March 5, 2020. https://www.stripes.com/news/veterans/after-years-of-failure-to-end-the-crisis-veteran-suicide-takes-center-stage-on-capitol-hill-1.621428.

Bowling, U. & Sherman, M. (2008). Welcoming them home: Supporting service members and their families in navigating the tasks of reintegration. *Professional Psychology: Research and Practice 39*(4), 451–458.

Braun, V. & Clarke, V. (2006) Using thematic analysis in psychology. *Qualitative Research in Psychology*, 3(2): 77–101. ISSN 1478-0887.

Brewer, B. W., Van Raalt, J. L., & Linder, D. E. (1993). Athletic identity: Hercules' muscles or Achilles heel? *International Journal of Sport Psychology, 24*, 237–254.

Brewer, B., Van Raalt, J., & Petitpas, A.P. (2000) – Self-Identity Issues in Sports Career Transitions. In D. Lavalee & P. Wylleman (Eds.), *Career Transition in Sport: International Perspectives*. Morgantown, WV: Fitness Information Technology.

Brockman, C., Snyder, J., Gewirtz, A., Gird, S. R., Quattlebaum, J., Schmidt, N., Pauldine, M. R., Elish, K., Schrepferman, L., Hayes, C., Zettle, R., & DeGarmo, D. (2016). Relationship of service members' deployment trauma, PTSD symptoms, and experiential avoidance to postdeployment family reengagement. *Journal of Family Psychology: JFP: Journal of the Division of Family Psychology of the American Psychological Association (Division 43)*, *30*(1), 52–62. https://doi.org/10.1037/fam0000152.

Browning, 2015 Brewer, B. W., Van Raalt, J. L., & Linder, D. E. (1993). Athletic identity: Hercules' muscles or Achilles heel? *International Journal of Sport Psychology, 24*, 237–254.

Brewer, B., Van Raalt, J., & Petitpas, A.P. (2000) – Self-Identity Issues in Sports Career Transitions. In D. Lavalee & P. Wylleman (Eds.), *Career Transition in Sport: International Perspectives*. Morgantown, WV: Fitness Information Technology.

Brinn, A. J., & Auerbach, C. F. (2015). The warrior's journey: Sociocontextual meaning-making in military transitions. *Traumatology*, *21*(2), 82–89. https://doi-org.lib.assumption.edu/10.1037/trm0000030.

Bulmer, S. & Eichler, M. (2017). Unmake militarized masculinity: veterans and the project of military-to-civilian transition. *Critical Military Studies*. doi: 10.1080/23337486.2017.1320055.

Burri, A. & Maercker, A. (2014). Differences in prevalence rates of PTSD in various European countries explained by war exposure, other trauma and cultural value orientation. *BMC Res Notes*. 2014; 7: 407. Published 2014 Jun 28. doi:10.1186/1756-0500-7-407.

Caddick, N., Phoenix, C., & Smith, B. (2015). Collective stories and well-being: Using a dialogical narrative approach to understand peer relationships among combat veterans experiencing post-traumatic stress disorder. *Journal of Health Psychology*, *20*(3), 286–299. https://doi.org/10.1177/1359105314566612.

Chaterjee, P. (2015). A chilling new post-traumatic stress disorder: why drone pilots are quitting in record numbers. *Salon Magazine*, 3/7/15.

Committee on the Assessment of Ongoing Effects in the Treatment of Posttraumatic Stress Disorder; Institute of Medicine. *Treatment for Posttraumatic Stress Disorder in Military and Veteran Populations: Initial Assessment*. Washington (DC): National Academies Press (US); 2012 Jul 13. 7, Treatment. https://www.ncbi.nlm.nih.gov/books/NBK201108/.

Creech, S., Swift, R., Zlotnik, C., Taft, C., & Street, A. (2016). Combat exposure, mental health, and relationship functioning among women veterans of the Afghanistan and Iraq Wars. *Journal of Family Psychology 30*(1), 43–51.

Davis, S. (2019). The new research about complex post-traumatic stress disorder. *Complex PTSD Foundation*. https://cptsdfoundation.org/2019/07/22/the-new-research-about-complex-post-traumatic-stress-disorder/.

Demers, A. (2011). When veterans return: The role of community in reintegration. *Journal of Loss and Trauma: International Perspectives on Stress & Coping, 16*(2), 160–179.

Forslund, A. & Lindblom, C. (2019). Israeli government accused of abandoning soldiers with PTSD. *The Guardian*. August 21, 2019. https://www.theguardian.com/world/2019/aug/21/israeli-government-accused-of-abandoning-soldiers-with-ptsd.

Friedman MJ. (2005). Veterans' mental health in the wake of war. *New England Journal of Medicine, 352*(13), 1287–1290. doi:10.1056/NEJMp058028.

Gallagher, B. (2016). *Burden of Proof: Veteran Frauds, PTSD Pussies, and the Specter of the Welfare Queen*. Critical Military Studies.

Giacomo, C. (2019). Suicide has been deadlier than combat for the military. *New York Times.* November 01, 2019. https://www.nytimes.com/2019/11/01/opinion/militarysuicides.html#:~:text=The%20latest%20Pentagon%20figures%20show,active%2Dduty%20members%20in%202018.

Giourou, E., Skokou, M., Andrew, S. P., Alexopoulou, K., Gourzis, P., & Jelastopulu, E. (2018). Complex posttraumatic stress disorder: The need to consolidate a distinct clinical syndrome or to reevaluate features of psychiatric disorders following interpersonal trauma?. *World Journal of Psychiatry, 8*(1), 12–19. https://doi.org/10.5498/wjp.v8.i1.12.

Goff, B. S. N., Crow, J. R., Reisbig, A. M. J., & Hamilton, S. (2007). The impact of individual trauma symptoms of deployed soldiers on relationship satisfaction. *Journal of Family Psychology, 21*(3), 344–353.

Grojean, M., & Thomas, J. (2005). From values to performance: The journey that changes the traveler. In A. Adler, T. Britt, & C. Castro (Eds.), *Studies in Military Psychology* (vol. 4, pp. 35–59). Westport, CT: Greenwood.

Grossman, D. (1995). *On Killing: The Psychological Cost of Learning to Kill in War and Society*. Boston, MA: Back Bay.

Gruber, J. & Johnson, S. (2019). *Jump Starting America: How Breakthrough Science Can Revive Economic Growth and the American Dream.* New York, NY: Hatchett Book Group.

Hillman, J. (2004). *A Terrible Love of War*. New York, NY: Penguin.

Hutchinson, J., & Banks-Williams, L. (2006). Clinical issues and treatment considerations for new veterans - Soldiers of the wars in Iraq and Afghanistan. *Primary Psychiatry, 13*, 66–71.

Hwang, E.J., Peyton, C., Kim, D., Nakamo-Sato, K., & Noble, A. (2014). Post-deployment driving stress and related occupational limitations among veterans of Operation Iraqi Freedom and Operation Enduring Freedom. *The American Journal of Occupational Therapy: Official Publication of the American Occupational Therapy Association, 68*(4), 386–394.

Junger, S. (2016). *Tribe – On Homecoming and Belonging*. New York, NY: Fourth Estate.

Junger, S. (2010). *War*. New York, NY: Hachette Book Group.

Kime, P. (2019). Military suicides reach highest rates since record-keeping began After 9/11. *Military News.* October 1, 2019. https://www.military.com/daily-news/2019/08/01/pentagon-reports-record-number-suicides.html.

Kintzle, S., Schuyler, A., Ray-Letoruneau, D., Ozuna, S., Munch, C., Xintarianos, E., Hasson, A., Castro, C. (2015). Sexual trauma in the military: Exploring PTSD and mental health care utilization in female veterans. *Psychological Services, 12*(4), 394–401.

Knox, K. L., & Bossarte, R. M. (2012). Suicide prevention for veterans and active duty personnel. *American Journal of Public Health, 102*(Suppl 1), S8–S9. https://doi.org/10.2105/AJPH.2011.300593.

Kukla M, Rattray NA, Salyers MP. (2015). Mixed methods study examining work reintegration experiences from perspectives of Veterans with mental health disorders. *Journal of Rehabilitation Research and Development*, *52*(4), 477–490. doi:10.1682/JRRD.2014.11.0289.

LaGrone, S., & Eckstein, M. (2020). Pentagon 'Very Concerned' with Military Suicide Trends; Effect of Pandemic on 2020 Rates Unclear. *U.S. Naval Institute News*. October 1, 2020. https://news.usni.org/2020/10/01/pentagon-very-concerned-with-military-suicide-trends-effect-of-pandemic-on-2020-rates-unclear.

Libin, A. V., Schladen, M. M., Danford, E., Cichon, S., Bruner, D., Scholten, J., Llorente, M., Zapata, S., Dromerick, A. W., Blackman, M. R., & Magruder, K. M. (2017). Perspectives of veterans with mild traumatic brain injury on community reintegration: Making sense of unplanned separation from service. *American Journal of Orthopsychiatry*, *87*(2), 129–138.

https://doi-org.lib.assumption.edu/10.1037/ort0000253.

Lopez, C.T. (2019). DOD Releases Report on Suicide Among Troops, Military Family Members. *U.S. Department of Defense: News Reform*. September 26, 2019. https://www.defense.gov/Explore/News/Article/Article/1972793/dod-releases-report-on-suicide-among-troops-military-family-members/.

Maddow, R. (2012). *Drift: The Unmooring of American Military Power*. Broadway Books. Portland, OR.

Marcia, J. E. (1966). Development and validation of ego-identity status. *Journal of Personality and Social Psychology, 3,* 551–558.

Marcia, F.R. (2018). Why do Israeli soldiers suffer from PTSD less than American counterparts? South Florida Sun Sentinel: Oct 17, 2018. https://www.sun-sentinel.com/florida-jewish-journal/fl-jj-israeli-soldiers-ptsd-american-counterparts-20181024-story.html.

Mockenhaupt, B. (2016). The stolen valor detective: Staff Sergeant Anthony Anderson's mission to name and shame people who pretend to be military heroes. *The Atlantic*: December 2016 Issue.

Monson, C. M., Taft, C. T., & Fredman, S. J. (2009). Military-related PTSD and intimate relationships: From description to theory-driven research and intervention development. *Clinical Psychology Review*, *29*(8), 707–714.

Myers, M. (2020). Soldiers and Marines die by suicide 50 percent more often than sailors and airmen, report finds. *Military Times*. April 28, 2020. https://www.militarytimes.com/news/your-military/2020/04/28/soldiers-and-marines-die-by-suicide-50-percent-more-often-than-sailors-and-airmen-report-finds/.

Petitpas, A.J., & France, T. (2010). Identity foreclosure in sport. In S. J. Hanrahan, & M. B. Andersen (Eds.), *Routledge Handbook of Applied Sport Psychology* (pp. 282–291). New York: Routledge.

Petitpas, A. J. (1978). Identity foreclosure: A unique challenge. *Personal and Guidance Journal, 56,* 558–561.

Phillips, D. & Arango, T. (2020). Who signs up to fight? Makeup of U.S. recruits shows glaring disparity: More and more, new recruits come from the same small number of counties and are the children of old recruits. New York Times: January 14, 2020. https://www.nytimes.com/2020/01/10/us/military-enlistment.html.

Richardson, L.K., Frueh, B.C., & Acierno, R. (2010). Prevalence estimates of combat-related post-traumatic stress disorder: critical review. *Aust N Z J Psychiatry*, *44*(1), 4–19.

Roh, S. (2012). Suicide prevention in the military. *Health & Mental Health Policy*.

Rosbach, M. (2020). Chronic environmental stressors, not combat exposure, biggest predictor of PTSD in Korean and Vietnam veterans. *Oregon State University: Newsroom*. March 2, 2020. https://today.oregonstate.edu/news/chronic-environmental-stressors-not-combat-exposure-biggest-predictor-ptsd-korean-vietnam.

Rozanova, J., Noulas, P., Smart, K., Roy, A., Southwick, S. M., Davidson, L., & Harpaz-Rotem, I. (2016). 'I'm coming home, tell the world I'm coming home' The long homecoming and mental health treatment of Iraq and Afghanistan war veterans. *Psychiatric Quarterly*, *87*(3), 427–443. https://doi-org.lib.assumption.edu/10.1007/s11126-015-9398-7.

Sayer, N. A., Noorbaloochi, S., Frazier, P., Carlson, K., Gravely, A., & Murdoch, M. (2010). Reintegration problems and treatment interests among Iraq and Afghanistan combat veterans receiving VA medical care. *Psychiatric Services*, *61*(6), 589–597.

Sayer, N. A., Carlson, K. F., & Frazier, P. A. (2014). Reintegration challenges in US service members and veterans following combat deployment. *Social Issues and Policy Review*, *8*(1), 33–73.

Sayer, N. A., Orazem, R. J., Noorbaloochi, S., Gravely, A., Frazier, P., Carlson, K. F., Schnurr, P. P., & Oleson, H. (2015). Iraq and Afghanistan War Veterans with reintegration problems: Differences by Veterans Affairs Healthcare User Status. *Administration and Policy in Mental Health*, *42*(4), 493–503.

Senecal, G., & McDonald, M. (2017). Mission completion, troop welfare and destructive idealism: A case study on the phenomenology of a combat veteran's social reintegration. *New Male Studies, 6*(2), 64–89.

Senecal G., McDonald, M., LaFleur, R., & Coey, C. (2018). The social vacuum & the loss of solidarity for veterans experienced in civilian reintegration. *New Male Studies*, *8*(1).

Shane, L. (2019). New veteran suicide numbers raise concerns among experts hoping for positive news. *Military Times*. October 9, 2019. https://www.militarytimes.com/news/pentagon-congress/2019/10/09/new-veteran-suicide-numbers-raise-concerns-among-experts-hoping-for-positive-news/.

Shay, J. (1994). *Achilles in Vietnam: Combat Trauma and the Undoing of Character*. New York: Simon & Schuster.

Shay, J. (2003). *Odysseus in America: Combat Trauma and the Trials of Homecoming*. New York: Simon & Schuster.

Shay, J. (2014). Moral Injury. *Psychoanalytic Psychology*, *13*(2), 182–191.

Shields, D. M., Kuhl, D., & Westwood, M. J. (2017). Abject masculinity and the military: Articulating a fulcrum of struggle and change. *Psychology of Men & Masculinity*, *18*(3), 215–225. https://doi-org.lib.assumption.edu/10.1037/men0000114.

Smith, W. Thomas. (2012, May 24). Running with a sledgehammer. *Victory Institute*. http://www.victoryinstitute.net/blogs/utb/2012/05/24/leadership-101-running-with-a-sledgehammer/#more-5141.

Stimkus, K., VanTil, L., & Pedlar, D. (2017). 2017 Veteran Suicide Mortality Study: 1976 to 2012. Charlottetown (PE). Veterans Affairs Canada, Research Directorate Technical Report; November 2017.

Tanielian, T. & Jaycox, L. (2008). *Invisible Wounds of War*. Rand Center for Military Health Policy Research.

U.S. Department of Veteran Affairs. (2016). Suicide among Veterans & Other Americans: 2001 – 2014. Office of Suicide Prevention: August 3, 2016. https://www.mentalhealth.va.gov/docs/2016suicidedatareport.pdf.

Vasterling, J., Aslan, M., Proctor, S., Ko, J., Marx, B., Jakupcak, M., Schnurr, P., Gleason, T., Huang, G., & Concato, J. (2016). Longitudinal Examination of Posttraumatic Stress Disorder as a Long-Term Outcome of Iraq War Deployment. *American Journal of Epidemiology Advance Access*.

Webb (1978). *Fields of Fire*. New York, NY: Bantam Books.

Yeager, D. E., Magruder, K. M., Knapp, R. G., Nicholas, J. S., & Frueh, B. C. (2007). Performance characteristics of the posttraumatic stress disorder checklist and SPAN in Veterans Affairs primary care settings. *General Hospital Psychiatry, 29*, 294–301. http://dx.doi.org/10.1016/j .genhosppsych.2007.03.004.

# Index

# About the Authors

**MaryCatherine (MC) McDonald**, PhD, is Assistant Professor at Old Dominion University. Her research lies at the junction of phenomenology and psychology. She also works in the philosophy of technology, specifically as it relates to mental illness diagnostics and treatment methods. She has recently published a book on the phenomenology of traumatic memory, as well as essays on the phenomenology of combat trauma and the history of posttraumatic stress disorder.

**Gary Senecal** received his PhD in Psychology from the University of West Georgia in 2015. He currently serves as Assistant Professor of Human Services & Rehabilitation Studies at Assumption College in Worcester, MA. During this time, he has various taught courses, including Psychiatric Rehabilitation, History and Theory of Psychology, Performance, Motivation, & Rehabilitation, Sports Psychology, Human Disability Across the Lifespan, Client Assessment, and Military Psychology—the Social Reintegration of Veterans. His research focuses on the phenomenological psychology of violence, the social psychology of violence, and the career transitions of individuals who have retired from or been deselected from careers that exposed them to regular violent endeavors (in particular, contact sport athletes and military veterans). He is a current member of the Army Reserves and resides in Worcester, MA with his family.

www.ingramcontent.com/pod-product-compliance
Ingram Content Group UK Ltd.
Pitfield, Milton Keynes, MK11 3LW, UK
UKHW041844031026
15587UKWH00003B/989

9 781498 591096